Do You Hear the Battle Cry?

An Essential Handbook for the Wives of Christian Men

by Karen Blake

Document Technologies, Inc.
491 South Dean Street
Englewood, NJ 07631
(201) 569-9600

Printed in the United States of America
ISBN 1-928870-11-2

DEDICATION

This book is dedicated to God, who
taught me what is written in the pages of
this book in the *secret place.*

You are my First and Greatest Love!

I love You, Lord.

Table of Contents

ACKNOWLEDGMENTS

I want to acknowledge Pastor Bill Wilson, whose simple yet direct words, "You need to write a book," resulted in *Do You Hear the Battle Cry?* Thank you for that and for the many years of support, encouragement and motivation. Once again, your making a difference in one life will affect the lives of many, many others.

———

Special thanks to Crystal Wacker who taught me the importance of prayer and also how to pray. Thank you for standing with me as a true friend for these many years.

———

I thank all the staff wives of Metro Ministries for their insight, openness, and honesty, for this book grew out of the discussions at our meetings! It has been my privilege to be with you, such an amazingly dedicated group of women. You all will forever hold a special place in my heart.

———

Thank you to the following people for their help in editing and publishing this book and for their constant encouragement: Jake Jones, Brett and Leigh Anne Monk, Judith Mair, Donna Mahoney, Wendy Dawson, Barbara Wallace, Mary Ellen Breitwiser, Lisa Dolab, Cheryl Salem, Helen Balzer, and Cathleen Kwas. You all are the best.

———

The **biggest thanks** goes to my husband Chris. You said before we were married that we would have an adventurous life. It's been all that and more! I honor and respect you and I love and admire you *exceedingly.*

Please Read This!

Throughout this book you will read the phrase "a man in the ministry". By this I mean a man who is advancing the kingdom of God in any way, not just a man in a full-time paid position in the church.

So whatever your husband does to serve the Lord, he is "in the ministry". Therefore, you are the *wife of a man in the ministry.* And this book contains an important message for you.

1

The Battle Cry

Sarah was a waitress. Her life was as normal as could be. Timid and a little naive, she spent most of her time thinking about doing her job and maintaining relationships with her friends. The last thing on her mind was being involved in a war.

Disturbing reports on the news talked about people who were getting killed, but Sarah didn't know these people so, initially, the reports had little affect on her. But soon the killings were getting closer to home. Before she realized what was happening, several close friends had died. Finally, for reasons completely unknown to her, a stranger walked up to her and pointed a gun right at her forehead!

These are the opening scenes from the movie *The Terminator*. The heroine of the movie, Sarah Connor, did not realize that she was in a key position. Her unborn son was destined to become the hero of an unseen war of the future, so the enemy was out to destroy her. If he could destroy Sarah, the battle for human freedom would be lost before it ever started.

Sarah was nearly destroyed because she didn't know someone was after her.

KAREN

Karen got married in her early twenties, bright-eyed and ready to serve the Lord with all her heart, soul, mind, and strength. She and her husband worked in the inner city and saw thousands of children and families come to the Lord. But Karen didn't realize she was in a key position. She didn't know that someone was after her. And because she didn't know, she was nearly destroyed. That Karen is me.

My husband Chris and I have worked at *Metro Ministries* in Brooklyn, New York, for the majority of years since the early '80s. Tens of thousands of inner city children have heard the gospel through the bus ministry and Sidewalk Sunday Schools that take place throughout the week.

While the oppressiveness of inner city life sentences a child to poverty, drugs, crime, and jail, the gospel gives them hope and frees them to live the life God has planned for them. As lives have been changed through the power of the gospel, the face of the city is changing. As a result of this success, *Metro Ministries* has been instrumental in changing the approach to urban ministries around the world. But there's been a price to pay.

CAUGHT IN THE CROSSFIRE

Over the years I've been cursed at, threatened, rocked, and egged. I have seen people shot and killed, robbed at gunpoint, and beaten up. I have witnessed riots in the streets. I have awakened to the sounds of breaking glass and screaming people trying to escape burning buildings. I've attended too many funerals to count.

My husband has been late for dinner—delayed because he was running into burning buildings and rescuing frightened and helpless people. When the church was fire bombed late one night, he drove burning buses out of the church parking lot in order to keep the rest of our church buses from exploding. I stayed in the car praying that I would see him alive again.

We've been caught in the crossfire as drug dealers shot at each other (they don't aim very well). One night a bullet came through the window of a van Chris was driving—missing him by mere inches. I've had to teach our children to look both ways—not only when crossing the street—but before coming out of a building so they won't get caught in a shoot-out.

But these are not the things that have almost destroyed me—these are only the physical attacks. What have almost destroyed me, my husband, and our ministry are the *spiritual attacks on our marriage.*

THE REAL ENEMY

The real enemy is not the drug dealers—they're just stupid. The real enemy is the one behind the drug dealers, the fights, the fires, and the shootings. He is determined to destroy our ministry. He's out to ravage *your* ministry, whether you live in the city, the suburbs, or the jungle.

There's nothing Satan would like to do more than get right in the middle of your marriage and cause damaging stress, strife, and total destruction. He seeks to and enjoys seeing you hurt, your kids damaged, and your husband out there on his own—but that isn't his ultimate goal. His ultimate goal is to destroy your *ministry.*

He wants to keep you and your husband from talking about Jesus! He wants to hinder you from being a positive influence in your church, your neighborhood, and your entire community.

HAVE YOU EVER BEEN TO A BOWLING ALLEY?

All of the bowling pins are aligned in the shape of a perfect 'v.' Great bowlers know what it takes to hit the front pin because its fall causes all the others to tumble. I equate Satan's goal to destroy marriages and ministries with a bowling match. All the pins are different parts of your life. The different pins are you, your husband, your kids, your ministry together, and your ministries individually, etc.

The front pin, however, is your marriage. Satan's goal is to take one ball and knock down all the pins. How is he going to do it? By hitting the front pin. If he can knock down the front pin in precisely the right way, all the other pins will fall. So he *aims* at your marriage. Now you know why all those crazy problems arise that have no explanation. Somebody's after you!

YOU ARE A TARGET!

This is an all-out WAR. Satan is doing everything he can to destroy those who are advancing the kingdom of God. He tries to bring down the ministers by destroying their marriages. If you and your husband are advancing the kingdom of God, then know this: YOU ARE A TARGET. Your husband is a target. Your marriage is a target.

But God is sending out a battle cry for women to rise up and fight for their marriages and their ministries!

The battle cry is a call to stand up and fight, to guard your husband and your ministry with the weapon of God's Word through prayer. It's a call to walk in strict obedience to God's commands for wives, even though the world and your own human traditions may disagree.

It's a call to stand strong in the face of opposition when your marriage and/or ministry look like they're over. It's a call to take your rightful place, to live and move in the strong position in which God has placed you. From this strong position you can see your enemy clearly, and you have the power, through Jesus Christ, to stand against and defeat anything he throws your way. You are also in a position to *go on the offensive* and cause the kingdom of God to advance GREATLY.

Because of this, Satan does EVERYTHING he can to get you to come down from your strong position. Don't do it.

THE SOUND OF THE BATTLE CRY

Maybe you've had an inkling, a prompting, or a gentle urgency that there's *something more* to being the wife of a man in ministry than you know—a feeling that you're supposed to be *doing something*. Maybe your husband is in a full-time paid position at the church, and you're at home with the kids. You know you have a part to play, but aren't quite sure what it is.

Perhaps you and your husband work at secular jobs and you minister to the people at your workplaces, but you sense there is more you need to be doing. Or maybe you work side by side with your husband in a ministry, but it just seems like you're missing something.

What you are sensing is the battle cry! You want to take your place, but you don't know what your place is.

In one way, we're all different. There is no set mold for a woman whose husband is in the ministry. All of us have our own, personal ministries that God has gifted us for and work He expects us to accomplish. In another way, we're all the same. We all have the high calling to uphold, push forward, fight for, and encourage the man we're married to. There's nobody assigned to do that for my husband but me. There's nobody assigned to do that for your husband except you! Realize the position you're in!

You can sit back and let the devil have his way. Your marriage can get walked on, your ministry stomped on. You can let the

Terminator destroy and kill you. Or you can say, "Not today, Satan. Not while I still have breath in my lungs. You're not taking me out. You're not taking my husband out. You're not taking our ministry out."

THE VIRTUOUS WOMAN

I believe that you, like me, want to be wise and productive with your life. You want to be a help—a treasure—to your husband. You can do these things by being a virtuous woman. *Who can find a virtuous wife? For her worth is far above rubies* (Proverbs 31:10 NKJV).

I used to think a virtuous woman was kind and sweet and got up early to make her family breakfast. But when I read the Hebrew translation of Proverbs 31, I learned that she is much more than this. The word translated *virtuous* in this famous Proverb is the Hebrew word *chayil*. The word *chayil* has to do with armies and fighting, power and might.

Chayil is translated "valiantly" in Psalm 108:13, *Through and with God we shall do valiantly, for He it is Who shall tread down our adversaries.* It is translated "valor" in Joshua 1:14 that speaks of *...mighty men of valor...*helping their brothers possess the Promised Land.

What has God promised you and your husband? What "land" has He assigned you to possess? Whatever it is, when you take your place as a virtuous woman, you are in a key position to tread down the adversary and possess the land. Your husband cannot do it alone. God is sending out a battle cry for you to rise up and fight.

Maybe you don't want to fight. Maybe you'd rather not tread down the adversary! You just want to have a nice, quiet life. I know what you mean. My stepfather was a Special Forces Green Beret, serving in both the Korean and Vietnam Wars.

Growing up, I heard lots of war stories and I had to watch all the war movies. It didn't take long for me to make up my mind that I didn't want any part of war. I was glad to be a girl so I couldn't be drafted!

I just wanted to have a nice life. I wanted to love and serve God with all my heart, soul, and strength, but I wanted to do it while everything remained nice, calm, and peaceful. But that isn't one of the choices.

I found out that if you don't fight, you die. Unfortunately, I failed to make this discovery until I felt like my marriage was just about over! I don't want it to take that long for you. You may not make it.

You may think that since you married a Christian man, everything will just be okay. But simply marrying a Christian is not the end. As the wife of this man, you have to take your place and fight the battle for your marriage, your husband, and your ministry.

Do not be afraid. A virtuous woman is a strong woman. You will have the victory!

In 2 Samuel 22:40 and Psalm 84:7 *chayil* is translated "strength." *I have pursued my enemies and destroyed them; neither did I turn back again till they were destroyed. And I have destroyed them and wounded them, so that they could not rise; they have fallen under my feet. For You have armed me with strength for the battle.... They go from strength to strength....*

I still wouldn't choose to take part in a physical war. I respect and honor the men and women in our armed forces who do. They fight in wars not knowing whether they will win or lose. They fight in wars unaware of whether they will live or die. This is not so with the spiritual war—we are already victorious! We know we're going to win because Jesus has already won!

SOMEBODY'S AFTER YOU

You're a target. Your husband is a target. Your marriage is a target. Satan wants to destroy you. But God is sending out the battle cry for you to rise up and fight, to do valiantly and tread down the adversary, and to help your husband possess the land.

You can be a virtuous woman to do just that. You can be a woman of valor, a valiant warrior. You can be a woman who recognizes her enemy and does not turn back until he is destroyed. You can receive your strength from God and go from strength to strength. This is what God has called all of us to as wives of men in the ministry. This is what He has called *you* to.

Pause for a moment and listen. *Do you hear the battle cry?*

2

The Weapon of God's Word in Prayer

You now realize that you are a target. You hear the battle cry. You want to fight, but do not know how to get up and do it. The weapon God has given you is His Word and you use this weapon in prayer.

For the first several years of our marriage, I can honestly say that I hardly prayed for my husband at all! If I did, it was something like, "Lord, I pray for my husband...um... I pray that You'll help him...and uh, that he'll have a nice day. Amen."

I noticed, though, that when my friend Crystal prayed, she prayed with power and authority. Her prayers seemed to move heaven and earth. The difference? She prayed the Scriptures. God's Word is powerful, and He says it will not return to Him void, but it will accomplish that which he sent it to do (see Isaiah 55:11). So I started praying Scriptures over my husband, our marriage, and myself.

And wow! What a change! The change was not only in my husband Chris, but also in me.

Many other women have had the same experience. I teach a workshop for all the wives who come to visit *Metro Ministries*. I tell them what I'm telling you today: pray Scriptures over your husband. Many of those who try it tell me the same thing, "I saw an immediate change!"

Stephanie was one of these women. Her husband David was struggling in ministry. He felt like he was on a roller coaster, sometimes up, but most of the time, down. Stephanie tried to encourage him, but it was to no avail. As time went on with no change, she worried and despaired over his ministry and even his life!

After her visit to *Metro*, she started praying Scriptures over her husband and his ministry. Her scriptural petitions released the power of God in Dave's life and he is much more balanced, able, and strong. Stephanie changed too. She has learned not to worry, but to put her confidence in God in every situation. God will be able to use them both mightily.

Another example is Kathy who, along with her husband Steve, volunteers at their church. They desired to be more involved in ministry in the future. Kathy was trying to convince Steve that they needed to invest money to make this happen. The more she talked about it, the more he resisted. Then she stopped talking and started praying Scriptures over him and the situation.

For the next two Sundays at church their pastor talked about investments. Then one of Steve's friends "suddenly" brought up the need to invest and gave Steve a book. Now he wants to invest and is excited about how this will enable him and Kathy to spend more time in ministry as they get older.

Your prayers have a big influence on what gets done in the world!

IT'S SIMPLE

Maybe you're like I was and never prayed the Scriptures before. It's really easy. Micah 6:8 NIV clearly details what the Lord requires of us. It's a good prayer to pray for your husband. The verse reads, *He has showed you, O man, what is good. And what does the Lord require of you? To act justly and to love mercy and to walk humbly with your God.*

So you would pray, "Lord, I thank You that You have shown us what is good. I pray for my husband now, that in all his dealings today, he will act justly. I pray that he will love mercy and show kindness to everyone he comes in to contact with.

"I thank You that You enable us to walk with You. It is such a privilege. I pray that my husband will walk humbly with You today, and when he lays down to sleep tonight he will know that he followed Your will and Your ways."

It's not your eloquence that produces change. It's the power of God's Word. Through your prayers, God will set your husband's steps in a straight line. He will restore broken parts of your relationship and prevent evil from getting the upper hand. It doesn't mean you won't struggle and suffer because God uses both of those for your good. It does mean that you and your husband will have the victory and fulfill the purpose for which God made you.

Let's try another illustration. In Ephesians 1:17-19 Paul details his prayer for the people in Ephesus. You can turn it into a prayer for your husband. "Lord, I pray that You will give my husband a spirit of wisdom and revelation. I pray that the eyes of his heart will be enlightened in order that he may know the hope to which You have called him, the riches of the inheritance You have given him, and the incomparably great power You have made available to him. Thank You that with this wisdom and revelation my husband will make good decisions today."

KEEP NOT SILENCE

Isaiah 62:6 says to put the Lord in remembrance of His promises and to keep not silence. Take your place. Get into your strong position. Search the Bible for God's promises and pray those Scriptures over your husband, your marriage, and your ministry each day. You will not only be defending your marriage and ministry, but you will also be causing the kingdom of God to go forward strongly. God's kingdom will advance as you believe and declare what He has promised.

"I thank You, Lord, that You who have begun a good work in my husband WILL continue it until the day of Jesus Christ! I thank You that he has the MIND OF CHRIST with creative ideas and solutions to problems and that he CAN understand what You are telling him. I thank You, Lord, that you infuse him with inner strength to FULLY ACCOMPLISH everything you have set before him to do today!" (Philippians 1:6, 1 Corinthians 2:16, John 10:4, Philippians 4:13)

Don't just stand there and take the blows from the enemy. He'll destroy you if you let him. God has given you everything you need for life and godliness and victory. Pick up the weapon of the Word of God and fight!

Note: *If you would like more help in praying Scriptures, get the book* **The Power of the Praying Wife** *by Stormie Omartian (Harvest House Publishers, 1997). It is made up of thirty, brief chapters, each dealing with the different parts of your husband's life. At the end of each chapter there is a powerful scriptural prayer—strong and to the point. The wives of the staff of Metro Ministries use it as a prayer handbook.*

3

Spiritual Discernment

God will give you discernment as to what you need to pray. Maybe you don't think you have discernment. You do! Ephesians 1:3 says that we have every spiritual blessing in Christ. One of these blessings is spiritual discernment.

Sometimes you will feel that something is wrong, but you don't know what it is. Do not ignore this feeling. It, in fact, is not a feeling coming from the realm of your emotions. It is the Holy Spirit prompting you to pray. Ask God how you should pray. Many times He will give you understanding about what you should pray. A Scripture will jump in your head. Don't wonder about it. Pray it.

At other times, though you feel the urge to pray and you ask God what it's all about, you won't know exactly. Pray in the Spirit in those times. *Likewise the Spirit also helps in our weaknesses. For we do not know what we should pray for as we ought, but the Spirit Himself makes intercession for us with groanings which cannot be uttered* (Romans 8:26 NKJV). I realize that "praying in the Spirit" means different things to different people. Whatever it means to you, do it.

God gives you spiritual discernment to detect problems before they come to fullness. Don't say, "Oh, look at that. That doesn't seem quite right. Hmmm. I'll bet that will turn into a problem...." Stop it right there, pick up your Bible, and pray-fight. Through your faith demonstrated in prayer, God will "nip the problem in the bud"—stop it before it comes to fruition. *"...If you have faith as a mustard seed, you will say to this mountain, 'Move from here to there,' and it will move; and nothing will be impossible for you"* (Matthew 17:20 NKJV).

THE IMPORTANCE OF DISCERNMENT

One of the strongest characteristics of *Metro Ministries* is the unity of the staff and the volunteer workers. It is the thing that people who visit here comment on the most. The staff and volunteers come from different countries, cultures, and denominational backgrounds, but we live and work in unity because we are all here for one purpose: to change a generation for Christ. I believe because of our unity, we have a strong anointing (see Psalm 133).

We are not to be ignorant of the schemes of the devil so that he does not get the advantage over us (2 Corinthians 2:11). We have unity. What is the devil going to try to do? It's simple. He's going to try to bring division. Time and time again I see division trying to come in. God gives me (and others) discernment to see it from afar.

Because my husband is a leader in this ministry, the enemy is going to try to bring division between my husband and the other leaders. He focuses his efforts on splitting the ministry right down the middle or breaking it up into many parts.

He works hard at this, because we are stomping on his territory daily. Every day, people are getting saved, delivered, and healed. I feel like the enemy is daily sending in more of his "troops" to tear us down.

So what do I do? I pray immediately when I detect any division. If Chris tells me about something someone said or did—even though it seems small—I pray. I declare Scriptures over the ministry. I don't say, "Oh, my gosh, we have to pray!" and act crazy or super-spiritual. But I lock it away in my head and when I am alone, I go to prayer. Time and time again the enemy's plans have been thwarted. And the kingdom of God continues to advance.

What makes your ministry great? What is God doing in your midst? Don't be unaware of the enemy's schemes! You can be sure that whatever is positive in your life and ministry is what the devil is after. He will attempt to destroy whatever makes your ministry great, and he will not stop trying. We need women who will not stop holding the line, pushing it back in prayer. God has already set us up to win the victory, but we must do our part.

4

The Enforcers

Now I rejoice in what was suffered for you, and I fill up in my flesh what is still lacking in regard to Christ's afflictions, for the sake of his body, which is the church.
—Colossians 1:24 NIV

The Apostle Paul tells us that he had to make up what was lacking in Christ's afflictions. How can something be lacking in Christ's afflictions? Didn't He pay the full price for our salvation, our deliverance, our healing, and our victory? Yes, of course He did. So what could be lacking in Christ's afflictions?

First John 3:8 NKJV says, *...For this purpose the Son of God was manifested, that He might destroy the works of the devil.* The word translated *destroy* is the Greek word *luo*. *Luo* means "to break, as in breaking a legal contract." God gave Adam and Eve dominion over the earth. When they sinned, they handed the dominion of the earth over to Satan. Jesus Christ came to break the legal contract that Satan has over the earth and all its inhabitants.

The work is already done for our salvation, our healing, our victory, and our freedom. But Satan is a thief and a destroyer and will get in anywhere someone is not enforcing what Jesus has done. In the strong position of wife, you have the power and authority to make up what is lacking in Christ's afflictions and to enforce what Jesus has already done for your husband.

HOW RIDICULOUS!

Imagine the owner of a jewelry store putting a sign in the plate glass window at night that says, "IT IS AGAINST THE LAW TO BREAK INTO THIS STORE AND TAKE THIS JEWELRY." He locks the door when he leaves for the night, but has no gates on the windows and no alarm system in place. What is going to happen? All the law-abiding citizens are going to respect the sign and obey the law. But the thieves are going to ignore the law, break in, and steal. Why? No one is enforcing the law.

The devil is a thief and a lawbreaker. If no one is enforcing what Jesus has done, then he just enters into a situation, wreaks havoc, and steals.

It's like the drug-free zones that surround the public schools in this country. On or near every public school there is a sign that says, "Drug Free School Zone." It means that you cannot sell or even possess drugs within one thousand feet of the school. In New York City, these zones "patrolled by signs" are particularly ridiculous.

There are drug dealers on many corners. Picture them out there, counting it off. "One, two, three," they say, walking slowly. "...Six hundred twenty-seven, six hundred twenty-eight, six hundred twenty-nine..." They are careful not to make a mistake.

"...Nine hundred ninety-nine, one thousand! ...Okay, boys, put the tape down here. We can't cross over that line when we sell our drugs." Do they do that? Of course not!

The "Drug Free Zone" is a law that people worked hard to put into effect. I remember when a man from Washington D.C. came and told us about it. He was so proud. He really thought it would make a difference. The reason the law and the sign make no difference—the reason it's so ridiculous—is that it is not enforced.

The drug dealers just laugh and ignore it. If the police were to be at the schools 24/7 and enforce the law, then the drug dealers would listen.

It's the same with the devil. If you are not operating from your strong position and enforcing what Jesus has already done, he will come in and steal. You need to be an enforcer. Enforce everything Jesus has done for your husband! If you see a work of the enemy in his life—discouragement, depression, despair, ungodly sorrow, confusion, overwhelming stress—kick it out. Those things are not allowed to be there.

Say aloud, "Discouragement, you may not be in my husband's life. I kick you out in the name of Jesus. The blood of Jesus has already been shed for my husband's freedom. The Word says that God is my husband's glory and the lifter of his head." (See Psalm 3:3.)

Once someone comes to enforce what Jesus has done, Satan must leave. He has no right to be there, but until that time he can wreak havoc, destroy, and steal. God put you in the strong position of wife to guard your husband from the wiles of the evil one and to enforce what Jesus died to give us.

STANDING AT THE GATE

In your strong position as the wife of a man in the ministry, you will not only kick *out* the work of the devil, but you will also invite *in* the work of the Holy Spirit.

Imagine that your marriage is a walled city with only one gate. Anything that comes into or out of the city passes through the gate. Your job is to guard the gate. The King gives you authority to remove or eject what is bad. You also get to invite in what is good.

Your prayers will be a combination of kicking out what is bad and inviting in what is good by the authority of the name of Jesus, and the power of the Word of God. Don't worry about the cost. The blood of Jesus has already paid it. It is an important job. You are in a strong position.

Let's use strife as an example. Peter says he has to go back to church again tonight. Shirley knows he has to go, but is angry inside because he hasn't spent much time with her and the kids. She mutters, "Okay, fine." But it's not fine, and when he comes home, she gives him the cold shoulder. What has happened? Strife has entered in.

Shirley is standing at the gate of her marriage and has authority over what goes in and out. Let's replay this scenario and see what Shirley can do differently. Peter says he has to go back to church again tonight. Shirley knows he has to go, but feels angry inside because he hasn't spent much time with her and the kids.

After he leaves, she gets alone for a minute and says, "In the name of Jesus I kick strife out of my marriage and out of my home. Lord, Your Word says that You give us peace and that whatever I ask for according to your will I can have. I give You all my negative feelings, Lord. I ask for peace in our relationship and in our home and thank You for it."

Peace is back in the home and back in her heart. Then she prays for God to change her feelings or her husband's, or both, and looks for God to work it out. As we will see in a later chapter, she will either need to stay quiet or talk to her husband about it. God will let her know. The important thing right now is that she took care of the strife AS SOON AS SHE COULD and did not let the devil get a foothold.

Take your position. Guard your marriage. Guard the gate. You are not alone. God is with you. Isaiah 28:5,6 says that the Lord

Himself **will be strength to those who turn back the battle at the gate.**

A WORD OF CAUTION

It is important to remember that your husband has a free will. Praying Scriptures over your husband releases the power of God to work in his life, but he can still choose to rebel against God and His ways. Do not even entertain the notion that it is your fault if you don't see fast changes, that you didn't pray enough, or that you don't have enough faith. All of those thoughts are lies from the enemy. He's trying to put you in bondage. Just keep on praying and trusting God. Sometimes it takes time.

Also, praying for your husband does not mean you to have control over him. Many times when you pray for your husband, God will show you ways that you need to change. Be open to that!

Note: *For more on the principles of intercessory prayer, I recommend the book **Intercessory Prayer: How God Can Use Your Prayers to Move Heaven and Earth** by Dutch Sheets (Regal Books, 1996).*

5

The Fierce Anger
of the Lord

If you're like me, you always heard the battle cry faintly off in the distance, but you didn't know what it was or what to do about it. You always felt this energy and "fight" in you, but you didn't know how to use it. What you have been sensing is the fierce anger of the Lord.

In Genesis 3:15, God says to the serpent, ...*I will put enmity between you and the woman....* The Hebrew word translated *enmity* has to do with hostility and fierceness. So the enmity or *anger* that God put between the woman and the serpent is a *fierce anger.* This fierce anger that started with Eve and the serpent in the Garden lives on in us today! God has placed it in us to use as a powerful weapon against the enemy.

This is good news! It means that when you see the work of the enemy in your husband's life—whether it comes in the form of discouragement, strife, division, pride, confusion or anything else—you don't have to just stand there, watching it happen. You can use that fierce anger that rises up in you, the holy anger of the Lord, to fight and defeat the enemy.

What does this fierce anger feel like? If you saw someone physically attacking your husband, you would become angry. Your heart would start beating faster, adrenaline would pump through your veins, and you would jump on the one attacking your husband. You would do something! Or, better yet, what if you saw another woman flirting with your husband? What would rise up in you? Fierce anger! You would do whatever it took to stop it. That's what fierce anger feels like!

Many of us were taught from the time we were little girls to not get angry. It's true that we should walk in love and gentleness toward our husbands and other people. But God gave us this fierce anger against Satan, and we need to use it. When something's going wrong and you feel holy anger rise up in you, don't try to suppress it. Let the zealous indignation of the Lord rise up in you against Satan himself. Take your weapons—the name of Jesus, the blood of Jesus, and the Word of God—and do battle against the enemy.

Then you can say with David, *"I have pursued my enemies and destroyed them; and I did not turn back until they were consumed. I consumed them and thrust them through, so that they did not arise; they fell at my feet. For You girded me with strength for the battle; those who rose up against me You subdued under me."* (2 Samuel 22:38-40).

Pursue your enemies in prayer. God will give you the victory!

AIM AT THE RIGHT FOE

This fierce anger God has given us is aimed at Satan. But Satan, the liar that he is, tries to deceive us into aiming it at someone else. Recently I saw a promotion for *The Bugs & Daffy Show* that illustrates this point. (Having a young child means that I watch a lot of the Cartoon Network!)

In the promo, you see the barrel of a shotgun in the foreground. It looks as if you're aiming the gun at Daffy Duck. But

Daffy draws your attention to an arrow-shaped sign pointing to Bugs Bunny. The sign reads, "Shoot him!" So the gun moves from aiming at Daffy Duck to Bugs Bunny. Then Bugs flips the sign around so that it points to Daffy Duck. The gun returns to Daffy Duck. It fires, and feathers fly everywhere. And, in classic cartoon style, as the smoke clears, Daffy is standing there burnt to a crisp.

How does that relate to prayer and the fierce anger of the Lord? Satan knows we have this fierce anger aimed at him. He knows he can't take it away from us. So, like Daffy, he tries to get us to aim at somebody else. And who would that somebody else be? Our husbands!

When everything is not "the Garden of Eden" at home, the devil (and our own flesh) entices us to "Shoot him! Shoot him!" and to use that fierce anger on our husbands. I think that when we do, the devil just sits back and laughs at us and at God. The devil really doesn't have to do anything. We are doing his work for him! (Ouch!)

Remember, **your husband is not the enemy**. Even when the worst problems arise in your marriage, the battle is not you against your husband. It is you, your husband and God against Satan.

Right now, let's flip the sign over. Let's aim the gun at the REAL enemy—and keep it there!

When your husband is acting like a jerk toward you, being rude or downright wrong, aim that fierce anger that rises up in you at the enemy of your soul—not at your husband. Say, "Satan, you will not have me, my husband, our marriage, his ministry, my ministry, our children, our home, nothing! For we are born of God, and the evil one cannot touch us (see 1 John 5:18)," and "I humble myself under Your mighty hand, God, and I thank You that you will teach me Your ways (see Psalm 25:9)."

Fire that gun at the real enemy and watch the feathers fly! Then God will step in and do what you cannot do. He will teach you His ways and cause you to have a right relationship with your husband. You will have the victory!

Maybe you're not violent by nature. Neither am I. But when I see the enemy come in and try to take what's mine, what is already paid for, what was purchased by the precious blood of Jesus, I get violent. I take that fierce anger of the Lord and aim it right where it belongs. Let's make sure that Jesus did not die in vain!

And from the days of John the Baptist until now the kingdom of heaven suffers violence, and the violent take it by force (Matthew 11:12 NKJV).

6

More Powerful Than Prayer

What is more powerful than prayer? Prayer combined with obedience. Prayer combined with obedience is more powerful than prayer alone, no matter how much fierce anger you have. Getting in line with God's commands makes your prayers more powerful. In fact, when you choose God's ways in combination with prayer, it actually makes *more power available*. James 5:16 says, *...The earnest (heartfelt, continued) prayer of a righteous man makes tremendous power available [dynamic in its working].*

You are going to need this dynamic power working in your marriage and ministry if you are going to accomplish all that God has for you to do. This power makes you able to stand on the heights. This power makes you able to stand in the evil day. This power shuts down the enemy. This power produces miracles. This power makes you and your husband able to accomplish all that God has set before you. You can have this power, IF you live according to God's ways *and* pray. *The earnest prayer of a righteous wife makes much power available.*

God has given you and your husband a great vision for your lives. If He hasn't, ask Him for one. God would not show you something that is not possible. It is possible! With God *all* things are possible (see Matthew 19:26 and Mark 10:27). But just as great as this vision is, the enemy wants to keep it from happening. You are going to need all the power available to succeed in your ministry and defeat the devil. God is willing to give it. Are you willing to do what it takes to receive it?

Disobedience and unrighteousness will stand in the way of receiving God's power. Disobedience makes it easy for you to be deceived. Unrighteousness gives the enemy a foothold. It's up to you. You must be determined to obey God's commands and His ways for wives. Then you will succeed. It's what God has called us to. It's what God requires for wives of men in ministry. Otherwise you'll lose.

DON'T BE CRAZY

In order for a soldier to be successful in battle, she must obey the commands given by the Commander in Chief. The commands are provided for her protection, provision, and power. They are given by someone who knows much more than she does—someone with vision enough to see the big picture. We would all agree that a soldier who refuses to obey commands as she goes into battle is crazy.

God is our Commander in Chief. We are in a war that we will definitely win, but we must obey His commands. To rebel, or say, "I'll take this command. It makes sense to me. But, no, I don't want that one," is crazy. There's no way you're going to win. The smartest thing you can do is to decide to obey God's commands no matter what the world says, no matter what your background says, no matter how much your soul protests. Make up your mind now that you will obey the Commander in Chief.

This is the promise for those who make this choice: *You shall establish yourself in righteousness (rightness, in conformity with God's will and order): you shall be far from even the thought of oppression or destruction, for you shall not fear, and from terror, for it shall not come near you* (Isaiah 54:14). You will stand in the evil day. Your marriage and your ministry will stand.

Isaiah 66:2 says that God will have *regard* for those who tremble at His word and revere His commands. When God has regard for you, you will surely win!

As you continue reading this book, look for God's commands. Line yourself up with God's ways for wives. It will make much power available, power that is essential to winning the war.

7

Respecting Your Husband

I had my life and marriage all worked out my own way. I had seen marriages go badly before, but I always thought it was because one of the partners was not a Christian. I said, "As long as I marry a Christian, everything will be fine. In fact, it will be more than fine. It will be wonderful!" Then I met Chris Blake. He was a wonderful Christian, already active in ministry and determined to follow God his whole life. We spent a lot of time together serving the Lord and became best friends. Then we got married.

"LORD, TEACH ME YOUR WAYS!"

For years after we were married I did things my own way—what I thought was right in my own eyes. I really believed that I knew what I was doing, but I kept falling flat on my face. When I realized my own ways weren't working, I cried out to God, "Lord, I don't know how to be married! I need help! Please teach me Your ways!"

So God started in. He dug deep. It was like God performed surgery on me. He exposed a lot of wrong thinking, pulled it out, and replaced it with the truth of His Word. He gave me my "marching orders!"

One command God gave me is very simple: Respect and reverence your husband. **Do it whether you think he's worthy of it or not.** That's it. No questions asked. No arguments. This is God's way, according to Ephesians 5:33, ...*and let the wife see that she respects and reverences her husband....* This is God's way for wives to act. It is exactly what I was asking Him for. But I had the world's way so ingrained in me that, when I heard this command, a shocked and rebellious attitude rose up in me. How about you?

Look at it this way. There are principles of life laid out in the Word of God. They are God's ways—how things work in His kingdom. These kingdom principles do not make sense to the world.

We'll use tithing as an illustration. The world says you have to keep all your money and make sure that you are taken care of. God says we need to give ten percent of our income to Him and that He will take care of us and give us everything we need. People in the world may say we're crazy. We reply, "You just don't understand."

The world says to be great, you must be in charge and tell everyone what to do. The kingdom of God says in order to be great, you must be a servant. People in the world may vehemently disagree, but we say, "You just don't understand."

The world says it's okay to have sex with whomever you want, whenever you want. We say, "No, that's not right. That's not God's way." When they laugh and say, "We're going to do it anyway," we feel sad for them knowing that they *just don't understand.*

But when the world suggests that we respect someone only when we think they are worthy of it, we jump in and agree! "Yes! You're right!" But that's not what the Word of God says. The Word of God says, ...*and let the wife see that she respects and reverences her husband.*

Do you see what is inherently wrong with respecting your husband only if you think he is worthy of it? It puts you in the position of the judge. "Let's see. According to my calculations, you don't deserve any respect today." It sounds like the Pharisees.

What does it mean "respect and reverence" your husband? And how can you do it? Let's look at Ephesians 5:33 again in The Amplified Bible. *...And let the wife see that she respects and reverences her husband [that she notices him, regards him, honors him, prefers him, venerates, and esteems him; and that she defers to him, praises him, and loves and admires him exceedingly].*

Let's take it apart, word by word, to understand exactly what God is commanding us to do.

I need to see to it that I notice my husband. Don't take your husband for granted. Notice him. Notice what he's doing. That's what you did when you first became interested in him. You noticed him. "Oh, there's that guy again. Look what he's doing. Isn't he cute?"

Your husband will always be growing and changing. Notice the new things he does or how well he does the old things. Don't miss the excitement of everyday life by looking only at the grand scheme of life and not the details.

I need to regard him. You probably have your own ministry. In one way or the other you serve the Lord through helping people. It is important to regard your husband more than the masses of people you minister to.

One simple way I do this is to make sure there is food in the house, especially the basic things like bread and milk. One day I was out "ministering" to someone. When I came home, I saw an unopened can of tuna fish and a jar of mayonnaise on the counter. I knew what that meant. There was no bread in the house! It was a small thing and, of course, Chris did not say anything, but I realized I had messed up. I should have made sure he was taken care of before I went out to take care of someone else. I regarded this other person more than I regarded my husband. That's wrong.

I need to see that I honor my husband. Honor your husband in front of your children and in front of other people. Honor him with your words and your actions. Honor him by not interrupting when he's talking. Honor him by not finishing his sentences.

Sheila realized that when she spoke to the president of her company, she did not interrupt him. She honored him. She waited until he has finished speaking before she responded. When Sheila saw that she was honoring her boss more than her husband, she quickly changed. Her husband Rick can now finish his sentences and he appreciates it!

Also, be proactive. Don't wait until your husband does something you think is honorable. Honor him and watch him become more honorable.

I need to prefer him. This one I love. Have you ever become so angry with your husband that you think, "Forget him! I'll just go out and find another man!" only to realize you would pick the same kind of man? Preferring him means that you realize out of all the men in the world you would pick him. You preferred your husband before you got married. You chose him. Nobody forced you to say, "I do." Prefer him now.

Let him know that out of all the men you know, you like him best. Let him know that out of all the men in the restaurant you're in, he's the best looking. Make yourself do it. Don't wait for happy, lovely, cute, little feelings to come sweep you away. God has given you this command to prefer your husband in order for you to win the battle and succeed over the long haul! Prefer him and let him know you do.

In order to do marriage God's way, **I need to see to it that I venerate my husband.** Although all the words we are looking at are synonyms for respect and/or reverence, *venerate* carries the meaning of "giving *great* respect and reverence for someone." You must greatly respect your husband. How do you do this—especially if you don't like the way he's acting? You can greatly respect him for the *position* he is in.

Galatians 3:28 says, *There is [now no distinction] neither Jew nor Greek, there is neither slave nor free, there is not male and female; for you are all one in Christ Jesus.* We are in an equal position at the foot of the cross. But so that there is order in the family, the husband is the head of the wife (see Ephesians 5:23).

Just like any other institution or organization, there has to be a head for the sake of order. A school needs a principal. It doesn't mean the principal is better than the teachers. The principal could do nothing without them. But the principal is positioned as the head. So it is in marriage God's way. The husband is the head of the wife and that position in itself deserves respect.

The President of the United States came to make a speech in the office building where my sister Leigh Anne works. Leigh Anne had not voted for this man and had little respect for him as a person because of his alleged immoral activities. To her surprise, when the President walked in, awe filled the room, and she felt an instant respect and reverence. For the man? No. But for the man in that *position.*

It is this same respect and reverence that we must have for our husbands, not because we approve of everything they do, but because of the position they are in.

Separate what your husband is acting like from the position he holds in your family. Venerate or greatly respect and reverence him because of that position he holds. Make it a decision of your will. Then you are placing yourself under God's almighty hand, because you are submitting to what God has set up. It shows your trust that God will help you, hold you up, and make your paths straight, and He will.

Life becomes a lot easier as a result of making the decision to reverence your husband's position in your home. Everything doesn't have to pass through your "strainer" so to speak. You don't have to judge every action and attitude and decide whether to respect or not. You just respect out of obedience to God and He takes care of the rest.

If your husband is a leader in the church, make sure you

venerate him for the position he's in. Don't become too familiar. When he's in the pulpit, it's best not to think of him as your husband. Think of him as God's man—His servant. Let God speak to you through him or you may miss out and even become bitter.

Yes, he can get up and preach with power and authority even if he wasn't a perfect man while you were at home an hour earlier. He still carries God's anointing.

I need to esteem my husband. When you hold someone in high esteem, you think highly of him or her. So esteeming your husband has to do with how you *think* of him. Watch your thoughts. Think on the good things.

This one you can't fake. You can't be apart from your husband all day, thinking poorly of him, and then respect him when you see him. The right words may come out, but he'll know you don't mean it.

The danger in spending years living closely with someone is that it is easy to take him for granted. Concentrate on the good things about your husband. Think positive thoughts *on purpose.* This is totally a choice. You can control it. Hold your husband in high esteem.

Philippians 2:3 NKJV says, *Let nothing be done through selfish ambition or conceit, but in lowliness of mind let each esteem others better than himself.* Esteem your husband as better than yourself. Think of him and his needs before you think of yourself and your needs. Ouch! Now you know why I said it was like God was performing surgery on me.

Sometimes we get into good and evil battles in our thoughts. It goes like this, "I know I'm right, and my motives are pure. I know I'm hearing from God on this. So he must not be hearing from God. He's just wrong. He must not have much of a relationship with God right now. I wish he could be more like me." In essence, you're saying, "I'm good and he's evil."

Oh, you're not saying it consciously. Nevertheless, it's there. I know, because I've thought that way before and, if I have done that, you probably have too. The only difference is that I have to confess my sin in this book and you get to repent silently!

Put on lowliness of mind. ...*Clothe (apron) yourselves, all of you, with humility [as the garb of a servant, so that its covering cannot possibly be stripped from you, with freedom from pride and arrogance] toward one another* (1 Peter 5:5). This way you can have proper thoughts about your husband. Why is this so important?

Number one, what you think affects how you act. Number two, what you think affects the way you pray. Keep your mind full of good thoughts for your husband, and there won't be any room for any bad thoughts!

In order to live God's way in my marriage, **I need to defer to my husband.** I can best illustrate this by using an "Alyssa story."

The other day, my daughter Alyssa was begging me to let her have a friend over. If you have children, I'm sure you know the drill. "Please, please, please, please, pleeeeeease, can I have a friend over? I don't have anyone to play with." Of course, her sad, yet precious, face and her big, brown, soulful eyes accompanied these words. Needless to say, I went and picked up her friend. After about a half hour of playing, they decided to watch a video.

Alyssa marched right into the kitchen where I was and, very disturbed, said, "She doesn't want to watch the same video I want to!" I told her, "You should let her choose." I explained to her that if she wants to *have a friend* she has to do what *her friend* wants to do much of the time.

I say the same thing to wives. "If you want to *have a husband,* you have to do what *he* wants to do much of the time." That's what it means to defer to your husband.

Alyssa isn't spoiled. She doesn't always get her way. But being the only young child in the family, she does get to pick what video to watch, what book to read, or what toy to play with. Perhaps we're like Alyssa. We beg to be married, and then when we get married, we still try to run our lives like we're single.

If you want to make all the choices, big or small, stay single.

But if you choose to be married, and you want your marriage to work, you must defer to your husband. This is God's way.

I need to see that I praise my husband. Tell him he's the greatest. Give compliments freely. Praising your husband is linked to the other parts of this verse we've already studied. For example: When you get into the habit of **noticing** your husband, then you can praise him with what you notice, "Oh, I noticed how you took care of that problem for me. Thank you."

Praising your husband with your words will **honor** him. Don't keep how you respect him to yourself. "You know, I really respect you for how you've been faithful to what God has called you to do. I know it's been hard."

As you **esteem** your husband in your mind, praises will flow out of your mouth because whatever you think automatically comes out in your words and in your actions. Tell him, "These girls are so blessed to have you as a father!"

Praise him in front of other people. Praise him behind his back. Praise him on purpose. Think of good things to say ahead of time. Wait for the right moment, and then speak! For example, if your husband is about to preach, lean over to him and tell him his sermon is really going to help a lot of people. Or right before your husband leads praise and worship, tell him that the way he worships God really inspires everybody. You know how to boost up your own husband. Do it!

Loves and admire him exceedingly. This one I had to think about. How do I love and admire my husband *exceedingly*? Especially in moments when I don't think he's worthy of it? When the feelings just aren't there? Am I just supposed to fake it and be ditzy and say, "Oooh! I love my husband!" while I'm angry (and a bit self-righteous) on the inside? No. God has a better plan.

I remember when Chris and I were engaged. I was so in love with him—so in love that I knew my rational thinking was affected. So during the last six months before we got married, I kept praying, "God, if you don't want me to marry Chris, please stop me." I knew that I was vulnerable at the time—my emotions were decidedly engaged. I was completely incapable of discerning any real problems, and I really trusted God to do whatever He had to do to stop me if the marriage wasn't right. He probably would have had to hit me over the head because I was blinded by love. I knew that if anyone would have come to me and said, "I think this will be a problem in your relationship," I would have said, "Thank you, but I'm not worried about it. I know *it will all work out!*"

Any potential problems that crossed my mind were easily dismissed with the same words, *"It will all work out!"* I loved and admired Chris *exceedingly.* And because God did not hit me over the head with a two-by-four or an iron skillet, I married him.

To love and admire my husband exceedingly today is a great key to cutting through what tries to weigh me down in my marriage. Please get this. It's a way to escape being bogged down. It frees you from your escalating thoughts like, "He said that, but he means this. And if he does this, then I'll do that. Then this will happen, and oh, there's no hope! Look at this big problem! We're headed for a divorce! What will we do about the kids? This is awful!"

One day, my thoughts were going just like that when I remembered God's command to respect and reverence my husband and, specifically, to love and admire him exceedingly. In my mind, I went back to our engagement days. Then I looked right at the problem at hand and said with a smile, "Oh, *it will all work out!*" It was as if the "problem" dissolved into thin air. I started laughing out loud. I was free!

Try it for yourself. The next time you feel weighed down by all the problems and impossibilities with your marriage and your personalities, think back to the attitude you had while you were still engaged and say with a smile, "Oh, this will all work out!" and it will! It's more than just not worrying. It's totally proactive.

RUNNING IN THE PATH OF HIS COMMANDS

If you feel stuck—like you're not going forward or going back, but you just kind of "are,"—check it out for yourself. Coming into line with this command of God to respect and reverence your husband will *unstick* you! If you feel trapped on every side, and you don't know which way to go, this is it. This is what you've been looking for.

The psalmist put it like this, *I will run in the path of your commands, for you have set my heart free. I will never forget Your precepts, for by them you have renewed my life* (Psalm 119:32, 93 NIV).

Obeying God's command to respect and reverence your husband sets your heart free from the bondage of bitterness and anger! It also sets your heart free to hear clearly from God. It allows you to receive correction from the Lord—which is mandatory for your growth. Essentially, respecting and reverencing your husband frees you from everything that is holding back all the blessings that God is longing to pour out on you. It truly renews your life!

Obey the command of the Lord! Respect and reverence your husband. Do it whether you feel like it or not. I'm not going to sugar coat it—*it will feel like you're dying!* Your flesh is not going to give up easily. But remember that it's just flesh. It hurts when it is dying, but once it's dead, it doesn't hurt anymore. So go for it.

REJECT THE WORLD'S WAY

Wherever you are in the world reading this, and whatever culture you come from, realize that in order to obey the Lord, you must drop the world's way of thinking and take on God's way. You can't keep the world's way and do God's will at the same time. You need to exchange one for the other.

In the United States of America and in many European countries, the world's way is feminism. In other countries like Mexico, the culture is strongly matriarchal. That means that the woman is seen as predominant in the family and society. While that is different than the countries where feminism rules, it is still a worldly culture, set up on worldly philosophies and human traditions. *See to it that no one takes you captive through hollow and deceptive philosophy, which depends on human tradition and the basic principles of the world, rather than on Christ* (Colossians 2:8 NIV).

Whatever your worldly philosophy is, wherever your human traditions lead you, you need to drop them. You are to be in the world, not of it.

How do you leave the world's way behind and switch to God's way? Repent. Confess your sin and then you will be cleansed. You must confess this disrespect for your husband as sin, and not say, "Oh, God already knows I didn't mean to, and He knows what a hard time I've been having. I was ignorant. I didn't know. I didn't realize I was so influenced by the world. I didn't realize I was in step with a worldly philosophy."

All that may well be true—it was for me—but you still need to confess it as sin and repent of it. Sometimes we are so used to God's forgiveness and His cleansing that we omit this step of repentance.

WRITE IT DOWN

I challenge you to write down on paper all the ways you respect your husband. When I did that, I was filled with awe—a reverential fear of God—and a new, godly respect for my husband. Do it, and you'll see what I mean.

Then write each word from Ephesians 5:33 that we discussed: Notice, Regard, Honor, Prefer, Venerate, Esteem, Defer to, Praise, and Love and Admire exceedingly. Next to each word write down how you are going carry that command out.

For example, "I notice that my husband always opens the car door for me, and I'm going to tell him I appreciate it." And, "I will regard my husband by leaving church when he's ready and not insist on staying longer to talk to my friends."

THE EXCITING PART

After I wrote down how I would respect my husband and put it into practice, I started going around my house when I was alone saying, "I respect my husband! I respect my husband!" It was not easy at first. I felt a lot of resistance. I don't understand it all, but I felt like I was shutting doors when I said it.

Then as days went by and I kept saying it out loud at home and in my head at church, I felt as though I was slamming doors shut. I learned that respecting your husband is tied into praying and spiritual warfare. I felt like I was saying to the kingdom of darkness, "This is not a way in for you anymore. You don't have easy access here anymore. I respect my husband!"

After a few more days, I started saying, "I bless my husband!" It just flowed out of my mouth. At that moment, my prayers changed. Instead of asking God for good things for my husband so he could be better "because he was such a mess," I asked God for good things for my husband as one I regarded, held in high esteem, respected, and honored.

Wouldn't God please bless him and give him all the things he needed for life and godliness as He had promised, and wouldn't God deliver him from any enemy that would come against him, according to His Word? Same words, but much different attitude. I think that since that day my prayers have accomplished more than they ever have.

My obedience in combination with prayer made much power available!

8

Submission Is Not a Four-Letter Word

*Wives, be subject (be submissive and adapt yourselves)
to your own husbands as [a service] to the Lord.*
—Ephesians 5:22

As a wife you are in a strong position. You may say, "It doesn't feel strong. I always have to do what my husband says. It's so hard to submit." But submitting to your husband is obedience to God, and whoever obeys God is strong.

Remember, the devil wants to get you out of your strong position. He is afraid of you because of the power that is available to you in Christ Jesus. He fears the fierce anger God has placed in you. He knows what you can do to him and his kingdom by enforcing what Jesus has already done. He knows what you can do to advance the kingdom of God by taking your place next to your husband. **HE IS TRYING TO GET YOU OUT OF YOUR POSITION.**

Satan realizes that he cannot take you out of the position God has placed you in, so he tries to get you to leave it yourself. How does he do this? He does it the same way he does everything—through deception.

The devil has worked very diligently over many years to set up a world system that tries to convince us that women are weak. This world system says that if we want to be strong, we have to stand up and *fight* like a man—not *submit* to a man. It says, "You had better be like a man or you'll get walked on." With these lies, Satan tries to get us to disobey God and come down from our position. Sadly, he doesn't receive much resistance from us.

Know this: You are no threat to the kingdom of darkness if you are not in your proper position. You are not dangerous if you are disobedient to God's commands. You will do no serious damage to the dark realm if you refuse to submit to and adapt to your husband. In fact, you are *in danger* if you do not obey, because you come out from under God's protection.

Don't fall for Satan's lies. When you submit to your husband, you are strong and secure because you are submitting to God. So how can you succeed at submitting without pulling your hair out?

The great news is that the same God who tells you to submit to your husband also gives you a tool for complete victory. That tool is prayer. Here's how to succeed.

You are engaged in an argument with your husband. You *know* you're right, and so you say, "Come on, God, You know I'm right. Jump in here and help me."

You wonder why He doesn't. I think it's because we tie God's hands by not doing things His way. In Deuteronomy 5:29 NIV, we see that God yearns for His people to obey His commands so that they can be blessed. *Oh, that their hearts would be inclined to fear me and keep all my commands always, so that it might go well with them and their children forever!* God wants to help us. He longs to bless us. But we must do things His way.

So instead of engaging in an argument with your husband, back off and submit to what he is saying. Then pray. When you submit to God like this, it lets God be God. It unties His hands. One of four things happens when you do this.

#1 GOD WILL CORRECT YOUR HUSBAND

God Himself will speak to your husband and correct him. I imagine it like this: Once I back off and give the situation to God, then His hands are "untied." He is then free to tap Chris on the shoulder and say, "Oh, Chris. I need to talk to you about this."

When I first started handling disagreements like this, Chris would come to me and say, "Are you praying about this? I'm totally changing my mind about what we talked about!" I would just shrug my shoulders and put on my most innocent look. From then on I hid my "praying wife" book (Stormie Omartian's *The Power of a Praying Wife*), and prayed incognito, because now I understood what a powerful weapon it was! (Just kidding!)

So the first thing that may happen is that God will correct your husband, and he will change his mind.

Carla's husband, Ray, is a pastor and travels quite a bit. One night at dinner he announced that instead of coming home for one day after a ten-day trip, he was going straight to his next speaking engagement. Carla told him she didn't think that was a good idea, because she and the kids needed to see him. But Ray dismissed her concerns and said that's what he was going to do.

Carla was angry and a little hurt. She wanted to keep arguing, but God was teaching her to submit and pray. She simply said, "Okay," and dropped the subject with Ray. Then Carla presented it to God, trusting that He would work out what was best.

That night there was a guest speaker at church. Out of the blue, he mentioned that before he ever accepts an invitation to speak at a church or conference, he tells the person who is inviting him that he has to first check with God and his wife, because he knows it's important to include his wife in making his travel plans. This statement had absolutely nothing to do with the man's sermon!

Carla wanted to bring this up to her husband after the service, but she resisted the temptation. The next day Ray told Carla he had decided to change his plans. Carla was able to respond with, "That's wonderful, honey. Thank you."

She didn't need to argue with her husband. She submitted and prayed, and God took care of it for her. Had she tried to do it by herself, even if her husband had changed his mind, strife would have probably come on the scene. But with God, there is no strife or sorrow, only blessing. *The blessing of the Lord—it makes [truly] rich, and He adds no sorrow with it...* (Proverbs 10:22).

#2 GOD WILL CORRECT YOU

The second thing that can happen when you back off and pray is that God will come and tap *you* on the shoulder and say, "You are totally wrong about this," and further, He'll explain why. This is much better than being wrong and making a fool of yourself.

Backing off and praying allows you to hear from God. When you are in the heat of an argument and your flesh is in an uproar, it is difficult to hear His still, small voice.

And with many men, when you insist that you are right and refuse to submit, they get fed up and say, "Okay, do whatever you want!" They back off from their position as head of the house because they are not going to fight you for it.

At some later date when everything's going wrong and you cry out to God for help, He'll finally get to show you how you were wrong. Actually, some people never even get to that point. They live in misery—blaming other people, and never even consider that they could have been wrong.

Believe me, it's much better to submit, pray, and let God correct you if He needs to. It saves a lot of heartache, embarrassment, and time!

#3 IT'S A NON-ISSUE

When you obey God by submitting to your husband and committing your situation to God in prayer, you may realize the issue wasn't an issue at all. It's a non-issue! It wasn't important and certainly not worth fighting over. Anyone who has been married a long time knows that, for your marriage to be successful, there is a lot of compromising involved—just giving up of the way you think things should be. Some things just don't matter. Submitting and praying lets you see which things these are.

#4 YOU NEED TO CONFRONT

When you submit to your husband and pray, you may find that you need to confront him. Yes, there are times for confronting your husband. But don't try to do it in your own strength. That will only lead him to reject what you are saying. He'll construct walls around himself very quickly and you'll be shut out.

Back off and pray. God will make it clear to you what you should say, when you should say it, and how. When you do it God's way, you may speak exactly the same words that you would have spoken on your own. But instead of the walls going up, it will be received like a kiss on his forehead.

Now I don't know exactly how it works. I just know it does!

A MATTER OF TRUST

How much stress could be avoided, how much wasted time being angry at each other could be averted if we would learn to submit and trust God to take care of everything! Perhaps you didn't realize it before, but it's really a *trust issue.*

Do you trust God that He will take care of you? Do you trust that He will not let you get walked on? I didn't trust Him for many years, even though I have been a Christian since childhood. I had seen bad things happen to women, and I thought the only way to avoid them happening to me was to always maintain control.

"Never totally depend on anybody"..."always have a Plan B in my back pocket waiting to go"...and "always have one foot out the door in case this situation does not work out," were my unspoken mottos. Submission was a scary thing.

It meant that I wasn't in control and someone could take advantage of me! As I learned to trust God and believe that He had my best interests at heart, I could submit to my husband, because I realized I was really submitting to God and trusting Him.

God will not let your foot be caught in a trap (see Proverbs 3:26). But you must do things His way. Otherwise, you're out there on your own. You limit God as to what He can do. God has ordered submission into our lives to help us.

Actually, women are better off than they may think! The Bible is clear that everyone must submit to the authority God has set up. God will correct everyone in this area. No one gets to be on their own—proud or self-contained! But whereas we women can have rebellion removed from us in the privacy of our own homes, a man's rebellion is often worked out of them in the public arena.

They are corrected at work in front of their peers or fail at their business or at a project until they finally humble themselves and submit. Thank God that He lets us be broken privately.

DON'T FALL FOR THE LIE

Don't fall for the devil's lie that submission to your husband is bad or too difficult. He just wants to keep you from operating in the strong position God has put you in next to your husband. Remember, along with God's command to submit is the tool of prayer. With obedience and the proper use of this tool, we shall have victory and go out and do valiantly against the enemy (see Psalm 108:13)!

9

Walking in God's Power and Authority

How you treat your husband affects your marriage. It also affects your personal ministry. If you want to fulfill your purpose on earth, keep climbing to new levels with God, and see His power manifested in and through you, you must walk in His power and authority. In order to do that, you cannot have any rebellion against your husband—or any spiritual authority—not even in your heart. The more of God's power you want flowing through you, the stricter the requirements. I learned this the hard way.

A couple of years ago, I was learning all about the ministry of deliverance. I was so excited about it. God had delivered me from rejection and the fear of man and had broken a generational curse of divorce off my life. I was excited to be a part of seeing other people set free.

One day I was angry and frustrated because it seemed as though Chris was going out a lot, and I was always "stuck at home" with the kids. I told Chris, "I want a turn to go out by myself and *you* stay at home with the kids!" Chris simply replied, "Okay." (Why did he have to be so nice when I was so angry?)

This "little" rebellious attitude was comparatively mild to how I had acted before, so I didn't think anything of it. I went out and had a great time.

But that night I had a dream. It was a bad dream. I was at my mother's house and all these demonic things were happening. People who had died were knocking on the door. I would open a closet only to find another dead person. They weren't coming after us, but they acted as though it was normal for them to be there. My fear kept increasing as I continually failed to make them comprehend that they weren't welcome there. They just would not go away.

Then I spotted a package of seeds on a shelf. The label on the package said the seeds were used for witchcraft. "Here's the problem, Mom," I said with a cocky voice. "Don't worry. I'll get rid of them." I was confident in my newfound knowledge of our power over the enemy.

I placed the seeds in an oversized pot to burn them, stirring them with a big spoon. Instead of burning up, they only increased. All the while, these dead people were running around everywhere. Thank God, I woke up!

Some dreams are bad, but then you wake up and it's over. But this dream stayed with me all day. Late in the afternoon, I went to my friend for prayer. I felt more peaceful, but still unsettled. I finally cried out to God, "What are you trying to tell me?" It was at that moment when I heard God's still, small voice. This was His reply: "Rebellion is as witchcraft."

Suddenly, I understood why I couldn't destroy those evil seeds and had no power over Satan. The rebellion in my heart—though it was a small amount to me—was like witchcraft. I learned a valuable lesson. *If you want to have victory over the devil, you can't be on his side.* Rebelling against your husband (or any spiritual authority) puts you on the devil's side. You will not have any victory against the enemy with rebellion in your heart. Just believe it. Don't wait for a horrible dream!

Maybe you feel stuck or frustrated in your personal ministry. The teaching, preaching, soul winning, or praying is not going like you think it should. Check yourself for rebellion against your husband. God will be glad to expose it to you so you can repent of it and be set free. *...Are you unmindful or actually ignorant [of the fact] that God's kindness is intended to lead you to repent (to change your mind and inner man to accept God's will)?* See Romans 2:4. Then you can move on to what God has for you!

Search me, O God, and know my heart: try me, and know my thoughts: And see if there be any wicked way in me, and lead me in the way everlasting (Psalm 139:23,24 KJV).

10

The Silent Killer

Satan is trying to bring down your marriage in order to bring down your ministry. Some of his traps are less obvious than others. Envy is one of the most subtle. Envy in marriage? Yes, and watch out for it. It's a silent killer!

Envy is one of those secret sins that can remain in you and your marriage yielding its damage for years. It lurks in the dark places of your heart and wants to stay hidden as it causes bitterness, anger, and strife, but it needs to be exposed. For too long there has been an underlying current of, "Oh, no, we're Christians. We're in the ministry. We're not going to talk about this."

We need to be talking about it. Envy in marriage can lead to bitterness, discord, and division. Envy in one woman can split the whole church! We don't have time to play games with it. The stakes are too high.

Search me [thoroughly], O God, and know my heart! Try me and know my thoughts! And see if there is any wicked or hurtful way in me, and lead me in the way everlasting (Psalm 139:23). May God shine His light on our hearts and expose the darkness. Let it be seen for what it is, dealt with, and removed. Then we will be clean and free.

A WASTE OF TIME

How much time is wasted being envious and bitter? How much rest do we lose? How many of us are physically sick because of this sin and we don't even realize we're doing it?

Stacy spent *years* envying her husband Rick, and it was killing her. They had worked side-by-side in ministry for more than twenty years. But it was Rick who had received most of the recognition and praise.

It's true that in most cases of couples in ministry, the man receives more attention...more praise. This can lead to anger, envy, and bitterness. The woman says in her heart, "When am I going to be noticed? I'm working just as hard (or harder)! What do I get for all of my labor? What about me?"

When Stacy was honest with her feelings and presented her complaint to the Lord, God told her to humble herself. *Humble yourselves, therefore, under God's mighty hand, that he may lift you up in due time* (1 Peter 5:6 NIV).

Why would God tell us that He would lift us up when we get down? Isn't that the problem—us being lifted up? It's a problem if we *want* to be lifted up. It's a problem if we feel like we *have* to be lifted up. But when you honestly say, "God, whatever You want, I'll do...I just want to love and serve You...nothing else matters beyond a relationship with You"—that's when God exalts you.

He lifts you up because, at that point, everything that comes out of you glorifies Him. This is everyone's purpose for being here. *Let them praise and exalt the name of the Lord, for His name alone is exalted and supreme! His glory and majesty are above earth and heaven* (Psalm 148:13)!

Now Stacy is free from envy. She is free to serve the Lord and use the gifts God has given her to help other people. She feels healthier than she's felt in years. She's full of joy! It doesn't matter to her one way or the other if she gets any praise or recognition.

GOD OPPOSES THE PROUD

If your husband receives a lot of attention and praise, pray for him! Pray that he will give all the glory to God and walk humbly before Him. ...*no flesh should glory in his presence* (1 Corinthians 1:29 NKJV).

Micah 6:8 says that God requires us to act justly, to love mercy, and to walk humbly before Him. I pray these scriptural words over my husband all the time—not only because it is what God requires—but also, while God gives grace to the humble, He opposes the proud (see 1 Peter 5:5). It is an awful thing to be opposed by God. Nothing works, and frustration is the result. Pray for your husband to walk in humility. It will be a blessing to him and to you!

THE SOIL OF LOW SELF-ESTEEM

Many times envy takes root and grows in the soil of low self-esteem. So it's important to be comfortable with yourself and with who you are in Christ. Just because you and your husband aren't receiving equal attention doesn't mean you aren't doing anything. Be happy with the fact that you are walking with the Lord and obeying Him. If you need anything else besides that, you're headed for trouble.

If it takes positive feedback for you to serve God, the devil will arrange it so that you get one of two things: no attention at all or negative feedback. He'll try to trip you up. He certainly doesn't want you to take your place and fulfill your destiny. He may not be able to keep you from being a Christian, but he will try to hold back your positive affect on others.

God gives each of us one life to live and a destiny to fulfill. The Bible compares our lives and destinies to running a race. Although you are running your race next to your husband and it often seems to be the same race, it definitely is not!

There are some things you can do that your husband cannot do and vice versa. Together you are a strong team and, many times, you are working toward the same goal, yet your race is separate.

Ephesians 4:3 says, *Be eager and strive earnestly to guard and keep the harmony and oneness of [and produced by] the Spirit in the binding power of peace.* You and your husband are one, but you're not the same. You most likely have different gifts and abilities that compliment each other.

Seek God to know what your life race is. It is never dull or boring. It is never second best. Perhaps you feel you're running a race against your husband, and you're coming in second. As hard as you try, you never get beyond second place. And since there are only two of you, it's really last place in your estimation.

I have struggled with this. As I started to write this book and do more public speaking, I heard a voice inside of me saying, "Don't be excited. Chris has already written several books. It's no big deal," and "Chris has already spoken to thousands of people. You're way behind. You'll never catch up." But then I realized that voice was not the voice of God.

Instead, God's Word tells me that I am responsible to do what He has put before me, and I am to do it with vigor and excellence. So that's what I'm doing. And I enjoy my life so much!!

LIVING VICARIOUSLY THROUGH YOUR HUSBAND

The other thing to watch out for is getting your sense of self-worth from what your husband does. Carmen was very interested in the great things her husband Tony was accomplishing. Carmen thought the "greater" Tony was, the more special she was. She always wanted to know how many people attended the conferences where he spoke, what great miracles occurred, etc. "My husband is BIG in God's kingdom!" she thought. "He influences so many people!" It made her feel special.

That's wrong in two ways. First, it's wrong because who you are is not based on what you do or what someone else does. It's also wrong because it puts pressure on your husband to be whom you expect and need him to be. Your husband has to be confident that you would still love and support him, be proud of and admire him whether or not he was serving in ministry.

It can also go the other way where you are envious of other women's husbands in your church or ministry. "Why does her husband get more attention than mine?" This is especially dangerous because it opens the doors for strife and division in a church. We get caught up in things that don't even matter. We really need to leave all that behind.

A LESSON FROM LEESHA

Neither Leesha nor her husband Tom were Christians when they got married. Leesha became a Christian first and then spent several years praying for her husband. In fact, her whole church joined with her in praying for Tom. As you can imagine, everyone was delighted when Tom gave his life to the Lord.

In the next few years, he received a great deal of attention from the people at church. He grew quickly in the Lord and took his position as spiritual leader in their family. At the same time, however, Leesha found herself with mixed feelings toward her husband.

It got to the point where she no longer wanted to pray with him or even go to church anymore. She found herself thinking that maybe she should just step back and do nothing, like he had done for years. These thoughts shocked Leesha and, during a time of seeking the Lord through prayer and fasting, God revealed to her the problem: ENVY.

Leesha had been the spiritual leader of her family for so long that she didn't feel important anymore when Tom took his place. She felt as if she had lost her identity. She was envious of her husband's position and all the attention he got.

She cried out to God, "Lord, I obeyed You. I kept praying and going to church with the kids. Is this all I get?" God's reply was simple, "You obeyed Me, and you were faithful. Your reward is that you have a husband who is taking his place. You need to back off and let him do it."

Upon hearing this, Leesha admitted her feelings of envy toward Tom and repented of her sin. She gave thanks to God (and still does) for a husband who has taken his proper spiritual position. Then when she concentrated on who she was in Christ and what new things God had for her to be and do, her joy came back. She still has it today.

Now both Tom and Leesha are doing great. Together they are leading a Sidewalk Sunday School ministry in their city. And Leesha has been able to help many other women in her situation.

I hope this story encourages you if you are one who is praying for your not-yet-saved husband. Keep praying! But there's also a message in there for everybody.

If you have taken the challenge to pray for your husband, marriage, and ministry, know that, most of the time, your prayers will be answered in the form of tangible changes in him that you can quickly identify. No matter where he is when you start, the change will always be toward your husband assuming his rightful place as head of the home. This is the place God has planned and prepared for him.

Don't be shocked and don't resist the changes. Don't let envy come in and steal years of your life when you should be rejoicing. The message God gave to Leesha is the same for all wives of Christian men, "Let your husband take his place, back off, and be thankful."

GOD HAS A RACE FOR YOU TO WIN!

God has great plans and purposes for you. He has set a race before you. Run that race to win. Holding onto envy and bitterness is like showing up at a long-distance race with your heavy coat, hat, and boots on. You won't win. In fact, you won't even get very far!

The only way you can win the race is to ...*throw aside every encumbrance (unnecessary weight) and that sin which so readily (deftly and cleverly) clings to and entangles us ...* (Hebrews 12:1).

Here are three simple steps to take in order to *throw aside* envy and bitterness:

1. **Be honest with yourself.** Bring your feelings to the forefront instead of trying to ignore them or cover them up.
2. **Be honest with God.** Confess your envy and bitterness as sin to God. Repent, and ask Him to take it out by the root.
3. **Focus on who you are in Christ** and on what He wants you to do in your life-race.

We all need to be on the lookout for envy. Watch for it. When it tries to enter your life (or reenter once you've kicked it out), say, "No! I'm not playing that game anymore!" This will make you so dangerous! It's the kind of talk that makes the kingdom of darkness shudder. And while it's busy shuddering, God's kingdom advances!

11

The Words of Our Mouths

Even so the tongue is a little member, and it can boast of great things. See how much wood or how great a forest a tiny spark can set ablaze!
—James 3:5

The tongue has the power of life and death ....
—Proverbs 18:21 NIV

As a wife of a man in the ministry, you are in a key position. You have the leader's ear. It doesn't matter if you want it or not. You've got it. You are going to use your mouth either to build this man up or to tear him down. You are going to use your tongue, that little member, to push the kingdom of God forward, or slow it down. It's up to you.

Every wise woman builds her house, but the foolish one tears it down with her own hands (Proverbs 14:1).

Here are seven ways to use your tongue wisely.

1. Speak well of your husband.

She opens her mouth in skillful and godly Wisdom, and on her tongue is the law of kindness ... (Proverbs 31:26). What do we know about laws? We know that they are always true. The law of gravity says that everything will fall to the earth. What goes up ALWAYS comes down.

Likewise, having the law of kindness on your tongue means that EVERYTHING you say will be rooted in kindness. Easy? No. Possible? Yes! Let's break it down into bite size pieces.

Speak only kind words about your husband *in front of your husband*. Don't say, "Oh, no! He can't do that! He's terrible at that!" It may be true that he can't do something, and he may agree with you and laugh along with everybody when you say it, but saying those words in front of other people tears him down. Make every effort to have the law of kindness on your tongue.

Do not *correct* your husband in front of other people. It's just rude. If you feel something he has said is inaccurate, speak to him about it in private or not at all.

Not only should you speak only kind words in your husband's presence, but also you should speak only kind words *about your husband when he's not there*. When your husband does something mean, stupid, or annoying—don't go around talking about it. Everybody does mean, stupid, and annoying things—including you and me! Let there be grace in your speech. By tearing down your husband, you're tearing your "head" off. Ouch!

The way you talk about your husband has a big effect on how people see him and what they think of him. Let's say you meet two women at a pastor's conference, Jenny and Penny. All of Jenny's comments about her husband are positive. She mentions what a great father he is to their kids. She tells how he's implementing a new discipleship program at the church and that it is going so well.

On the other hand, all Penny has to say about her husband is negative. She lets you know that he's *always* late for dinner, that the church is running down his health, and that he just won't help her around the house.

What do you think of these two men? It's not a trick question. You think well of Jenny's husband and poorly of Penny's husband—before you even meet them! Does this mean that Jenny's husband is never late for dinner and that Penny's husband is a rotten father? No, but the information the two women *chose to say* affected the way you see their husbands.

Chris talks about our family a lot when he's preaching. I feel like everyone thinks good things about us because he never speaks an ill word. I remember a guest speaker that Chris and I took out to dinner who was the same way. Throughout the whole evening he spoke well of his wife; he talked about what a great cook she was and how she's always learning about different cultures. Everything he said about her was positive. By the end of the night I held her in high esteem and wanted to meet her. Is his wife a perfect person with no human frailties? No, none of us are, but her husband spoke so well of her that I already respect her!

From listening to you, WHAT DO PEOPLE THINK ABOUT YOUR HUSBAND?

Her husband is respected at the city gate, where he takes his seat among the elders of the land (Proverbs 31:23 NIV). Why is the husband of the virtuous woman respected at the city gate? His wife speaks well of him! Is this man without weaknesses or problems? No. (And truly, if your husband is living in outright rebellion to God his sin will find him out and he will not be respected no matter how much you talk well about him.) But love covers a multitude of sins. The virtuous woman does not go around spreading the "Bad News"! She chooses to talk about the good. She *chooses* to talk about the good. She *chooses to talk about the good.* ...You can too!

There is something to be said about the power of suggestion. When you choose to talk about the good things about your husband, others hear it and believe it. And, listen to this—your husband hears it and believes it too. Then he does more good because that's who he believes he is. *For as he thinks in his heart, so is he* ... (Proverbs 23:7).

Please understand that I'm not saying you should never talk to someone about a problem you're having. I'm not at all for covering up problems and acting like everything's fine. What I am saying is that you shouldn't talk about it to EVERYBODY.

Find a close friend that you can talk to. Choose this person wisely. It should be a godly woman who will guide you, pray with you, and not take sides. Pray and God will provide this person for you. Anything we ask according to His will shall be done. Also, seek to be this person for somebody else.

Maybe you can't find a friend nearby or feel uncomfortable with developing close relationships in your church because your husband is the pastor. Invest some of your money in long distance phone calls to someone that you are close to. Or make e-mailing a regular part of your day. Having a friend that you can talk to is *that important*, and is well worth the time and money you spend.

2. Speak life to your husband.

Death and life are in the power of the tongue ... (Proverbs 18:21). Are you speaking DEATH or LIFE to your husband? You say, "Why don't you come home?" and "Why don't you spend time with me?" Maybe your husband doesn't want to be around your MOUTH.

When he's home does he hear whining and complaining? Does he hear how he's not meeting your needs? Or are you like I used to be—saying the right words, but having an accusing tone in your voice? "No, no, that's okay. Don't worry about me." If your answer is yes to any of these questions, you need to change.

As hard as I tried, I couldn't get rid of that accusing tone of voice—until I made God my Source. Realize that He is the only One who can meet your emotional needs. Go to Him with your needs. If you do, then that "you're-not-meeting-my-needs" tone of voice will be gone! When you receive fullness of life from your heavenly Husband, you will be able to speak words of life to your earthly husband.

3. Use your tongue to confront wisely.

Submitting to God and doing things God's ways in no way makes us weak or wimpy. Sometimes we need to confront our husbands about a certain issue. Here's how to do it.

Pray first. Anything spoken out of anger or out of the flesh will not work. Following the flesh always leads to death. When you pray, give God time to show you any underlying anger and/or unrepented sin in your life. Then receive from God what you should say. Ask Him to show you the right time, and when He does, speak!

Do not worry about your husband's response. He may not—and probably won't—turn to you in slow motion, like in the movies, and say, "Oh darling, you are so right," and give you hugs and kisses. In fact, he may act as if he didn't even hear you or he may just give a grunt, but the scientific fact is that the airwaves carried what went out of your mouth into his ears. After you say what you have to say, drop it. Let God do His work.

4. Avoid being a "last word freak."

If you always have to be right and prove to your husband that you're right, you're going to have problems. Say what you have to say and then stop. For me, this took a ton of self-control, biting my tongue, walking out of the room, or singing a song, but the results are worth it. Now it is something we laugh about.

The basic principle is, "You can give up your 'rights' a lot and be married or you can be right all the time and be single."

5. Realize men and women communicate differently.

When I told Chris the subject of this chapter, I asked him what his advice to women about their words would be. He replied, "The fewer the better."

A traveling evangelist was at our church and he spoke very highly of women in his sermon. For about an hour after the service, he gave me much Biblical insight into the role of women and specifically wives. Then I asked him, "What is the one thing you think men want their wives to know?" His answer? "Don't talk so much."

The fact is that women use more words in a day than a man does. There are some exceptions to this rule, but generally it is true. So let's not fight it. Let's not argue about it. Let's find a solution.

One solution is to get a girlfriend that you can talk to! Chris used to give me a hard time about being on the phone an hour or more with my friend. Then I told him that if I didn't use all those words on her, I'd have to use them on him. Now he doesn't say anything and he's very grateful that I have a friend to talk to!

6. Guard your mouth. Don't say whatever is on the top of your head.

Your husband will go through difficult times. To everyone else, he'll seem okay, but to you he will show discouragement, frustration, anger, doubt, confusion, etc. When he expresses these feelings, you have an opportunity to help him, but you can't just say whatever is on the top of your head.

If you respond too positively, he may understand it to mean, "She doesn't understand me," or "My feelings must not be valid." He may withhold his feelings from you and even go to another for encouragement.

The other way to respond is to join him in his negativism. I tried that. It doesn't work. Your husband stays down and then you're down too!

I was really having trouble in this area and then I came across Proverbs 21:23, which says, *He who guards himself and his tongue keeps himself from troubles.* I asked God to please put a guard over my mouth so I wouldn't just say the first thing that jumped into my mind. He did, and now I am very careful to not say words that just come from me.

Words that come from my flesh are like nothing; they carry no weight. I have to go to God and receive from Him, then I will have words of life for my husband. Therefore, your personal walk with God is crucial because it is not just about you. It will determine how much you can help your husband.

Also, each man is different and has unique ways of dealing with stress. Most men know what they need when they feel these different pressures. They've been the same way since childhood. So at a time when he's in a good mood, ask him how he wants you to respond when he's going through a hard time. It will cut down on the guessing and you will be an effective encourager.

7. Take your role as encourager to your husband seriously.

You have a big influence on your husband, and if your husband influences others, realize that you are in the position of influencing an influencer. You carry a lot of weight!

My biggest contribution to *Metro Ministries* is to take care of my husband, to minister to him, to speak words of life to him, to serve him, and to pray for him. Then he can fulfill his duties properly and with excellence and with joy. This is a blessing to him and the entire ministry.

If I don't drive my bus, someone else will. If I don't visit the kids on my route, someone else will. If I don't make videos about the ministry, someone else will. But if I don't speak words of life to my husband, no one else will—at least not in the same way that I can.

The same is true for you. God chose you for your husband. You're the best one in the whole world to help that man you're married to. It is an awesome privilege and an awesome responsibility.

God placed us in this important position and gave us this special job. No wonder the enemy tries so hard to pull us away from doing it. However, if we submit to God and resist the devil, he will have to flee. Then we will use our mouths wisely to uphold our husbands and push the kingdom of God forward *strongly*!

12

Be Involved in Your Husband's Ministry

One way to protect your marriage from the enemy and advance the kingdom of God at the same time is to be involved in your husband's ministry. If you are together in thought and purpose you will accomplish much and it will be harder for you to be pulled apart.

This does not mean you have to work side by side with your husband. If he is in full time ministry and you stay home with the kids or work a secular job, that's fine. Follow what God leads you to do. If your husband leads a Bible study during his lunch hour at work, you're probably not going to be there. That's okay. What's important is your attitude. You have to have the desire to be involved and you have to do something with that desire.

HAVING THE DESIRE

Check yourself. If you have no interest in what your husband is doing, you're headed for trouble. The Bible says that wives should *adapt* themselves to their husbands as a service to the Lord. (Ephesians 6:22) You are not single any more. You do not have your complete independence anymore. Your life is not your own. Maybe that's not what you think you "signed up for", but it is! (To the single women reading this: Don't get married until you are ready to adapt. Don't get married until you are willing to give up some of your "rights".)

I have seen women pull their husbands right out of full time ministry after a couple years of marriage because they expected their husbands to adapt to them instead of the other way around. The ministry life could not provide the "standard of living" that they wanted and with relentless pressure (in ways only we women can do), they pulled their husbands *out* of what God put them *into*. That's dangerous business! Have enough sense not to do that.

By the way, you *can* raise your kids well in the city, or the jungle, or wherever God tells you to go. Your family is much better off in the middle of God's will than in a place that you think is "safer" or "better" for your kids.

Maybe you never realized that it is a command of God to adapt to your husband. However, now that you know that you need to, the feelings just aren't there. Honesty is good! Confess this to God and He will help you. Pray something like this: "Lord, I don't have the desire, but I want to obey your command to adapt to my husband. Create in me a clean heart and renew a steadfast spirit within me. I lay down my desires. Place Your desires in me." A broken and contrite heart He will not despise. He will place in you the desires you need.

DOING SOMETHING WITH THE DESIRE

Once you have the desire to do be involved in your husband's ministry, you need to do something with that desire. How do you know what to do?

One way is to listen to your husband. If you bombard your husband with questions, he may not talk, but at those times when he opens up on his own, listen.

Listen and then do. Maybe he says he hates making the overheads of the songs for Praise and Worship. Make the overheads for him. Maybe he says he wishes he could show appreciation to the volunteers somehow. Buy little gifts for him to give out. Maybe he's frustrated because he doesn't have time to pick up the props for Children's Church. Pick them up for him. If your gift is teaching, offer to teach a class for him. If your gift is talking, volunteer to make calls for him. Many times you will be gifted in areas where your husband is not. This is God's design. He will be glorified as you work together as one.

DON'T GET CAUGHT IN A TRAP

You are a unique person and so is your husband. That means that there are endless ways for you to be involved. You do not have to do what your friend is doing and you don't have to do what you think other people think you should do. If you try to copy what works for someone else, you will get discouraged. If you try to please other people you will end up in misery.

The bottom line is that God will teach you in the way that you should choose when you reverently fear and worship Him. (Psalm 25:12) Fear and worship the Lord and trust Him to lead you in what you should do. God is the Creator and He will give you creative ideas for your particular situation. Ask and you will receive!

Brenda's husband Alex drives an eighteen-wheel truck as his ministry. They have a small child and there is no way she can travel with him, but God showed her a way to be involved. Before every trip Brenda watches the Weather Channel and lets her husband know what to expect. When Alex returns, Brenda calculates the miles he traveled and types up his report. I doubt

Brenda loves to watch the Weather Channel, but she loves her husband and adapts to him as a service to the Lord. She is a wise woman.

GO WITH THE FLOW

One more thing you need to know: your role changes as you go through the different stages of your life. It's okay. For example, when you have your first baby, things will change. The amount of "outside the home" ministry will change! It's okay. God will give you new ways to be involved in your husband's ministry. Maybe your youngest child enters school and you start working outside your home. You will go through change. It's okay. God is the God of all the seasons of our lives and He will lead the way!

We adopted our daughter, Alyssa, when she was five months old. SUDDENLY, my life changed. I kept my Saturday Sunday School bus route, but immediately pulled out of the youth ministry and picking up people for church on Sundays. I started working part time and no longer attended staff meetings. I couldn't help Chris in all the ways I used to, but God had a plan!

Without me even asking for it, God gave me a ministry of prayer for my husband and his ministry. I had plenty of time to pray—when I was washing the dishes, doing the laundry, and making dinner. It let me play an important part.

Whether he says anything or not, your husband will appreciate it when you help him. He will depend on you. Proverbs 31:11 says of the virtuous (chayil) woman: *The heart of her husband trusts in her confidently and relies on and believes in her securely, so that he has no lack of [honest] gain or need of [dishonest] spoil.*

Be a wise and virtuous woman. Take your place and be involved in your husband's ministry. You will be building your marriage and advancing the kingdom of God at the same time!

13

Providing a Refuge

It is crucial that your husband has a place to relax, recover, and receive from God. You will be serving your husband and advancing the kingdom of God by providing a refuge for him. Your home can be a wonderful refuge for your husband. You, yourself, can be a great refuge for him as well.

A PLACE CALLED HOME

Make your home—whether it's a house, an apartment, a one room dwelling, or a hut in the jungle—a place your husband wants to come home to. Make it a place where he can relax and be himself. Take time to decorate it and make it as nice as you can within your means. God will inspire you as to how to make your home a refuge for your husband—He's very creative!

Saundra had always decorated in the colors and style she liked, never thinking about what her husband Paul liked. He said he didn't care. As God started teaching Saundra about making her home a refuge for her husband, she changed the color scheme and style to what she knew Paul felt comfortable with. She threw out of all the mauves and blues and used greens, browns and rusts.

Paul liked books, so Saundra had bookshelves built in the living room. Saundra loves it, not only because it looks nice, but also because she knows she created a refuge for Paul. Now everyone who walks in their house comments on how warm and cozy it is and how it is such a *refuge* from the harsh streets of the city where they live and minister. I guess God knew what He was doing!

LIVE IN PEACE

Make every effort to live in peace with all men ... (Hebrews 12:14 NIV). You will have to fight for peace in your home. Strife is crouching at the door ready to come in as soon as the door is open just a crack. Work at having peace. Allow at least fifteen minutes after you come back together at the end of a workday for a problem-free zone. Don't mention any problems that you've had during the day during this time. Don't hit him with, "The toilet's backed up, the kids are fighting, and the car has a flat tire," when he walks in the door. He won't want to come home anymore.

Trina, whose husband Frank was an associate pastor at their church, had quit her job to take care of their two kids. She always tried to impress Frank by looking busy when he came home so he would think her work was important too. This plan backfired on her as Frank looked more and more depressed each time he walked in the door.

Trina laid down her insecurities and started concentrating on making her home a pleasant place to be when Frank walked in. The changes were simple. She taught her children to run to him and say, "Daddy's home!" with lots of hugs and smiles for him when he walked in the door. Trina stopped cooking, greeted him with a hug and kiss and always had something positive to say. This made a big difference and now Frank says his favorite time of day is when he walks in the door of his home!

Take a minute to think of how your husband pictures your home. What does he think he'll find when he gets there? Is he glad to walk in the door? What are some simple changes you could make?

YOU CAN BE A REFUGE

Not only can you make your home a refuge for your husband, but you can also make *yourself* a refuge for him. Please understand—God is his Refuge. You're not taking God's place, but rather, you are letting God meet your husband's need through you.

Your husband not only needs a safe *place*, but also a safe *person* to come home to. He needs someone to accept him and love him. He needs someone to listen to him if he feels like talking and he needs someone he can just be quiet with if he doesn't feel like talking. You must be a safe person with whom he can share all his dreams and thoughts as well as his concerns and doubts and not have any fear of you repeating it or looking down on him.

Most men do not like to be barraged with questions. If you ask too many questions, many times your husband will clam up. Don't say, "Okay. Sit down right here and tell me about your day." Wait until he offers.

Be ready to listen to your husband. Sometimes he will start talking about what's important to him or what's bothering him when you are busy doing something else. Make every effort to stop what you are doing and give him the attention he needs when he needs it. He will confide in you things that no one else knows and you will have the opportunity to lift him up and encourage him. This is crucial in advancing the kingdom of God.

Do not demand to know everything that is going on in the church, even though your itching ears want to hear it. Chris protects me by not telling me all of the "junk" that goes on. This comes back to bless him because even if there's some big problems, he comes home to me and I am not affected by them. I am a refuge for him. If I know everything, I will be dragged down every time he is down and possibly be affected by a spirit of offense. Then who will lift him up?

At first I used to feel bad because I didn't know everything. People would say to me, "Oh, you know about so and so and so and so." "No, I don't," I'd say. (They would keep on talking to me like I knew anyway!) Then I realized I didn't need to know certain things that I couldn't do anything about.

You can say, "Well, I need to know *everything* so that I can pray for the people." If you ask God to give you His burdens so that you can pray about them, you will be praying for those people because they are on God's heart. That's what I do. Many times God leads me to give a word of encouragement to someone who has just messed up. I would not be able to do that if I knew everything going on in the natural because my own flesh would get in the way and I may add my own ideas and judgments.

All of us are in different positions. In some situations you may be able to say out of a pure heart that you really do need to know everything that is going on, or the position you are in requires you to know everything because you're the one that is assigned to deal with it. If this is true for you, then make your home a "no talking about problems in the church zone", or set aside a certain time to talk about them and make the rest of the time "off limits". Please heed this warning. If you leave talking about problems unchecked, it will grow out of control, take over all your time together and come back and bite you in the end. You will have a house full of strife.

There will always be problems in the ministry. Guard your home. Keep it as a refuge, not as an extension of the church office.

SENDING YOUR HUSBAND TO THE ROOF!

The opposite of being a refuge for your husband is to be a nag. Nagging will send your husband to the roof. *It is better to dwell in a corner of the housetop [on the flat oriental roof, exposed to all kinds or weather] than in a house shared with a nagging, quarrelsome, and faultfinding woman* (Proverbs 21:9).

Nagging usually takes place in the first few years of a marriage when you think everything will be or must be like the family in which you were raised, or that everything should be the way you envision it. You're trying to fix everything to the way it should be, *and why won't he cooperate?* Don't worry. That will change. As long as you are flexible and you are willing to let go of many of your "should-be's", you'll be fine. (See Chapter 19.)

Meanwhile, if your husband says you nag, you probably do. You probably don't see it. I didn't. Just ask God to help. He will show you how to fix it. You'll fix it and move on.

Sometimes your husband will withdraw "to the roof" and it's not because you're nagging. It's just what men do. If your husband is distant from you, not talking much, and/or sleeping on the couch for a few days, and God hasn't shown you anything you need to change, don't worry about it! That's what men do! He'll be back!

SETTING THE TONE

The woman sets the tone in the home. Peace, joy, and love in your home come from you and from your relationship with God. Your home, your refuge, is what you make it.

Likewise, the woman sets the tone in the church. Whether your husband is the senior pastor, the children's pastor, the youth pastor or a volunteer leader in the church, you set the tone for the area he oversees. Whether you like it or not, whether you want the responsibility or not, when you walk in, the room changes. Does it change for better or for worse?

You have tremendous power to influence people just because of whom you are married to. One encouraging word from you causes people to hope in and act on what God is telling them. At the same time however, one discouraging word from you, or even a discouraging look, brings people down. I don't know why. It's just part of God's design.

When you walk into the church, people will want to talk to you. People will want you to pray with them. People will be watching you and taking their cues from you. If you're excited about a ministry opportunity in the church, they will be too. It's just the way it is. Be prepared when you walk into the church to lift people up, to have a positive word, to have a smile. It will go a long, long way.

Sarah, whose husband was a pastor, didn't want this power and responsibility. She thought that if she denied and rejected it, it would not be there. But she was wrong. I wish this story had a happy ending. It doesn't. She soured everything that went on in the church with her bad attitude. Now her husband is not even a pastor.

Angela, on the other hand, realized that this extra influence was a gift from God and used it wisely. She kept encouraging everyone even when she was down herself. (She found that when she took care of the needs of God's people, He took care of hers!) Angela was always excited about all the church ministries, even though she was only involved in a few of them directly. She always had something positive to say. Today Angela and her husband are having a tremendous influence in their city through their exciting, growing church.

You can be like Sarah or Angela. It's your choice.

Be very careful, then, how you live—not as unwise but as wise, making the most of every opportunity ... (Ephesians 5:16 NIV). As the wife of a man in the ministry, you have a great opportunity to provide a refuge for your husband as well as to influence the people in your church for good. Don't miss it! Use the gift God has given you for His glory and for the building up of His kingdom.

14

Standing Strong in the Face of Opposition

Good is looking for *chayil* women. He is looking for women who will totally rely on Him and not faint. He is looking for women who will keep on fighting and never give up. He is looking for women who will stand strong in the face of opposition even when their marriage and/or ministry looks like it's over.

I believe you are that kind of *chayil* woman. You are strong in the Lord and He has put you in a strong position. No matter what, don't come down from your position!

What causes you to lose your position of authority? You lose your position of authority when you give it to the devil. You step down from your strong position when you agree with the enemy, when you give up, and when you say, "I've had enough. I can't do this any more. This is too hard." Satan barrages you with temptation to step down. Don't go for it.

This will be the hardest thing you ever have to do. DO NOT STEP DOWN.

God needs *chayil* women who will stay in their place and

guard their position. I remember one time when I was ready to give up. I was having thoughts like, "Maybe I'm just not meant to be married. Maybe I'm just not meant to be a minister's wife." Instead of resisting these thoughts, I entertained them.

Usually God speaks to me in a still small voice. This time He didn't. This time I heard the inaudible yet thundering voice of God command me, "Guard your position! Stay in your place!"

... Be strong, do not fear; your God will come, he will come with vengeance; with divine retribution he will come to save you (Isaiah 35:4 NIV). God will always come and rescue you, but sometimes there are other things that have to be worked out. Sometimes there is a period of time where you have to stand without much encouragement from anyone except what God has put in your heart.

At times like this, do not go by outward circumstances or appearances. Go by what God has put in your heart. Your marriage is not over. Your ministry is not over. Hold the line. Keep speaking scriptures over your husband, your marriage, your ministry. Do not give up.

This life, as the wife of a man in the ministry, requires you to live by faith. It's worth it. You may see many difficulties, but you also get to see God MIGHTY IN POWER. You get to see God's GREAT DELIVERANCES. You get to see His STRONG ARM!

The next three chapters are on standing strong in the face of opposition. Chapter 15 is about when times of darkness come...and they will. Just as the night follows the day and then the day comes again, your husband will go through times of darkness. You'll find out what to do during those times.

Chapter 16 focuses on when the unthinkable happens...adultery, abandonment, addiction. Guard against these things, but if they happen, don't give up. You can make it.

Chapter 17 deals with getting the most out of a difficult situation. If you have to go through a hard time, you might as well get something good out of it!

When opposition to your marriage and ministry comes, STAND STRONG. The Lord is with you! *[And indeed] the Lord will certainly deliver and draw me to Himself from every assault of evil* (2 Timothy 4:18a).

15

When Darkness Comes

Do not be alarmed when your husband is in a time of darkness. Do not be afraid. Do not be discouraged. A pastor or other Christian leader will go through many times of struggle and darkness. These struggles may be more intense and more often than what you would consider normal. This can bring confusion. "If we're living for God, why are we experiencing so many problems?" It's actually part of the position God has put your husband in as a teacher, leader, pastor, and/or motivator of His people!

It's good to know that God will not give your husband more than he can handle, but please know that He *will* bring him right to the edge. Sometimes you'll be the only one to see it. At church he seems fine and "on top", while at home he's suffering. It's okay. With God's help you can handle it. God wouldn't have put you in the position of his wife if you couldn't handle it.

WHY, GOD, WHY?

If you know the reasons why the dark times come, it will be a lot easier.

First of all, as a pastor or a Christian leader, your husband will go through trials for the sake of the people. Your husband will experience certain situations and feelings and hardships not for his sake, but so that he can understand what the people are going through and so he can hear from God as to how to deal with it.

Then, if your husband is a praise and worship leader, he can lead the people in true worship of God, no matter what the circumstances. If he's a pastor or teacher, he can teach the people how to handle difficulty. Chris says that he can tell what will be happening with the staff and the congregation in the next couple of months because of what he is going through now. Certain things about God are learned only in the dark times.

Dear friends, do not be surprised at the painful trial you are suffering, as though something strange were happening to you (I Peter 4:12 NIV).

But if we are troubled (afflicted and distressed), it is for your comfort (consolation and encouragement) and [for your] salvation ... (2 Corinthians 1:6).

Secondly, for your husband to be used by God in a great way, he must go through times of testing and breaking. God will search him, expose what doesn't belong, and require him to die to self. It won't be easy.

YOUR JOB

Your job during the dark times is to keep praying for your husband and to not become discouraged yourself. This is a good time to pick up *The Power of the Praying Wife* again and pray the prayers that God leads you to. It will encourage you. Remember, God is your Light. He illumines your darkness. *Though I sit in darkness, the Lord will be my light* (Micah 7:8b NIV).

Sometimes your husband will want you nearby and you can help. Other times he will be distant and it will be hard because you feel like you can't help. Don't succumb to your feelings. Our emotions often want to jump out front and lead the parade, but they are not able to lead. Make your mind, will, and emotions—the three parts of your soul—submit to God. (See Psalm 62.) You can be confident that God is having His way. He's doing His work.

TEMPTATION

Know that during the dark times, your husband will be tempted to walk away from God or to sin. God is not tempting him. It's just that in the dark times it is easy to be drawn away. *But every person is tempted when he is drawn away, enticed and baited by his own evil desire (lust, passions)* (James 1:14). Hold him up. Pray that He will continue to walk with the Lord and that nothing will be able to drag him away. Pray that the Lord's counsel shall stand in his life and that the Lord will do ALL His pleasure and purpose. (See Isaiah 46:10.)

The most important thing to know is that **the darkness will pass.** As surely as the night comes, the day will come. The night will not last forever. Hold on. Stand firm. Keep speaking scriptures over your husband, your marriage and the situation.

Light arises in the darkness for the upright, gracious, compassionate, and just [who are in right standing with God] (Psalm 112:4).

God has equipped you to stand strong in the face of opposition. When you got married He placed within you what you need to be a comfort to your husband in the dark times and not be dragged down yourself. Do not leave your strong position to entertain worry or doubt. Stand strong on the promises God has given you and your husband. The Lord girds you with strength (*chayil*)!

16

When the Unthinkable Happens

Satan wants to bring down your marriage in order to bring down your ministry. Know that your marriage is subject to attacks of the unthinkable. Atrocities like adultery, abandonment, and addictions will not only damage your marriage, but they also will damage many people in your church. Let us not be ignorant of the schemes of the devil! If he can cause one of these things to happen, he will!

During these times of difficulty, stand strong. The devil will try to make things look so bad that you give up. He will do *anything* to get you to believe him and step down from your strong position. Don't do it! Hold your position! God intends for you to have victory!

ADULTERY

The first thing to realize is that it can happen to you. As a Christian leader your husband is in a prime position to be drawn away by an adulteress woman. Why? There are many hurting women in your church. Some of them may be having a hard time with their husbands. They see that yours is compassionate and caring. Other women are attracted to men in power. They like the leader they see in your husband. Still others like to see whom they can get. It's nothing more than a game for them—the higher the man in leadership, the greater their sense of victory. Any of these women may go after your husband. *For the lips of a loose woman drip honey as a honeycomb, and her mouth is smoother than oil* (Proverbs 5:3).

Simone, who is a wonderful, strong Christian woman now, said that when she first went to church, she was checking out the men. She didn't care if they were married or not. If she wanted him, she was going after him. You may have grown up as a Christian, or just sheltered, and didn't know this went on in church. It does. Another woman will be happy for you to take care of your husband's laundry and children while she takes care of your husband's body and soul.

You must be wise and guard your relationship. Notice I said "wise" and not "scared". This is not something to be scared about, or hypersensitive, but the Bible says we are to watch and pray. The enemy usually comes in the door you're not watching.

WHAT TO DO

If there is a woman you feel is after your husband, talk to your husband about it. Ask him to make it point to stay away from her. A young woman named Kimberly came to me frustrated because a woman in her church was flirting with her husband. Kimberly asked him to stay away from her, but he just laughed and said she was being ridiculous.

If this is how your husband responds, don't be discouraged. Make it a matter of prayer and God will cause him to see what you see or at least respect your wishes. He will learn to trust your women's intuition and discernment.

Another thing you can do is to become friends with the woman yourself. Then talk about you and your husband. Sometimes this will make a woman who is after your husband back off. If she doesn't, you probably need to say something to her. I say "probably" because there's no hard and fast rules to this. God will lead you. The point is that you are not without resources and solutions. You do not have to sit back and watch it happen.

By the same token, you have to be willing to respect your husband's wishes if he says he's uncomfortable with a relationship you have with a man. Christina found this out when a male friend of hers gave her perfume for Christmas. She didn't think anything of it, but her husband Brad did and insisted that she give it back. She thought that it was ridiculous and told him so. "Now you know how I feel when you talk to me about staying away from certain women," he said. "Oh! So that's how it feels!" she thought. Christina quickly agreed to give the perfume back. As soon as she did she had this overwhelming sense of being protected from danger.

GUARDING YOURSELF

Men aren't the only ones who run off with someone! How do you guard yourself from having an affair? Be careful of close friendships with men.

Caroline's sister Erica was having problems in her marriage. Everything wasn't "happily ever after" at the moment. She started casually talking to a man at work. Of course, he was wonderful and understanding.

As each day passed, Erica felt closer to him and more distant from her husband. By the time Caroline noticed what was going on and warned her sister, the relationship had gone pretty far. Even though it wasn't sexual, the emotional ties were strong. Erica and her husband are still together, but a lot of damage was done. Why? Erica wasn't guarding herself.

It is difficult to work at a marriage that seems hopeless, but the blessings of God are delayed or even forfeited if we try to take care of our emotional needs ourselves and outside of God's ways.

If you are going through a difficult time, you may be tempted to think, "Forget this. I'll just go find another man who will treat me right, one who will meet my needs." It may make you feel better to think it or even say it to a close friend. Be careful! Even though you may have no intention of actually doing it, you are giving the devil a foothold when you think it or speak it out. If you continue to entertain these thoughts, the devil will certainly supply you with a man to "take care of you." Don't get down from your strong position.

Finally, even if both you and your husband know a relationship is totally innocent, be careful. As a leader, you must live a life that is above reproach. (See 1 Timothy 3:2.) Rumors can damage your reputation and your ministry. Stay far away from the edge.

AS IT IS IN YOUR HEART

If your husband does commit adultery, or starts taking drugs, or says he doesn't love you anymore, or anything else that hurts you terribly, then seek God and do what God puts in your heart to do.

We all know that Joshua and Caleb were the two spies out of twelve who brought back a good report about the land of Canaan. Actually, all twelve of the spies brought back a good report about the *land*, but Joshua and Caleb were the only ones that brought back the report that they knew with God's help, they were well able to *take the land*. In the face of terrible odds and bad circumstances, they had a good report.

In Joshua 14:7, Caleb says that he brought the report about the Promised Land *as it was in his heart.* God speaks to us through His written Word and He also speaks to us in our hearts. *Caleb acted on what God put in his heart and he received what God promised.* The others died in the wilderness!

Esther, a woman who visited *Metro Ministries* recently, told me that after several years of marriage, her husband left. One year went by. All of her friends told her to forget about him. Two years went by. They urged her to divorce him. Three years went by. They said, "God's got a great man out there for you." She answered, "I know God has a great man for me. It's my husband." God had put it in Esther's heart that she needed to wait and pray for her husband to come back.

After four years apart, Esther's husband came back! They have a wonderful relationship now and her husband now leads a ministry that helps young men at their church. Esther, like Caleb, acted on what God put in her heart and received what was promised.

If the unthinkable happens, check your heart. IF GOD PUTS IT IN YOUR HEART TO STAY WITH YOUR HUSBAND, THEN STAY! It doesn't matter what has happened, if God puts it in your heart to stay, then stay. If God puts it in your heart to wait for him, then wait. If God puts it in your heart to live with him and love him unconditionally, then do it! Don't worry about what everybody else is saying. You know what the Lord has put in your heart.

In no way am I suggesting that if you are in physical danger that you should stay. You can be apart physically and still be waiting and praying while your husband finds the help he needs.

ACCORDING TO YOUR FAITH

In Matthew 9:27-29 we read the account of two blind men. I believe that God had put it in their hearts that Jesus would heal them. That's why they pursued Jesus shouting loudly for mercy. "Do you believe that I am able to do this?" Jesus asked them. "Yes, Lord," they answered. Jesus touched their eyes and said to them, "According to your faith, be it done unto you."

Jesus is saying that to you today. "According to your faith, be it done unto you." When God gives you a promise about your marriage you hold on to it. You believe it. You speak it out. Keep on believing until you see it come to pass. Don't let doubt ROB you. The devil wants to destroy your marriage. God wants to heal it and build it and make it strong.

Marriages do survive adultery! Marriages do survive pornography! Marriages do survive drug addictions!

My friend Teresa and her husband James were busy serving the Lord in their church. But one day everything changed. James went back to his drug habit that he had before he was a Christian. Since then he has been in and out of jail and his life has been a mess, but God put it in Teresa's heart that James would one day be a pastor. The Lord confirmed this to her with two prophetic words given by people that didn't even know the situation.

Whenever I talk to Teresa on the phone and ask her how things are going, she says, "Oh, Pastor James? He's in jail right now, but I believe God's having His way in him and he will be a pastor just like God said." Teresa's not living in a fantasy land. She's taking care of her son and making necessary adjustments, but God has put a promise in her heart and she is choosing to believe it. I believe Teresa will receive exactly what God has promised. (As soon as James becomes a pastor, I'm going to print a new edition of this book with the victory report, so watch for those new editions!)

What does it feel like when God puts something in your heart? Sometimes it feels like a command. Sometimes it feels like an urging. Sometimes it feels like an encouragement. Most of the time it will feel like all three at once. It's what you know God is telling you in your inner most being.

Checking your heart is different than checking your emotions. Your emotions cannot be trusted. They are up one day and down the next. Truly, during a difficult time your emotions are down most of the time, but faith doesn't come from the realm of your emotions. Faith comes from the realm of the spirit. It is the ... *substance of things hoped for, the evidence of things not seen* (Hebrews 11:1 KJV). Go with what God puts in your heart.

Jeremiah 17:7,8 speaks about the person who trusts in the Lord. *He shall be like a tree planted by the water that spreads out its roots by the river... It shall not be anxious and full of care in the **year of drought** ....* (emphasis mine) Here's something you may not want to hear. You may be in for a *whole year* of drought. You may be in for *four years* of drought—not a drought with God, a drought in your relationship with your husband. But you can make it!

Sometimes we think, "Oh, this will be over in a week or two. This will be over in a month. I can make it." But is that really trusting the Lord? God convicted me that it wasn't. Trusting the Lord means saying, "Lord, I REALLY hope this is over SOON, but if it's not, and even if I have to live the rest of my life like this, then I trust in You. I know that you have an abundance of grace to give me the victory...one day at a time!"

DON'T GIVE UP

What therefore God has joined together, let not man put asunder (separate) (Matthew 19:6b). This is a scripture that is important throughout your marriage, not just at your wedding. I pray it like this: "What God has joined together let no man, no other woman, no human weakness, no desire of the flesh, and no demon from hell put asunder!" Draw the line with your prayer. Mark the boundaries with your prayer.

One of the biggest lies the enemy tells us is that we are stuck, that there's no way out, that there's no hope. He's hoping we'll believe the lie so we'll give up. He's hoping we'll believe the lie and get down from our strong position so that we'll stop bothering him!

The truth is we are never stuck. No bad circumstances ever last forever. In fact, one of the things we can count on in life is that things always change. But when you're in the middle of a battle, especially where your emotions are severely wounded, it can seem true. "You're stuck and nothing will ever get better."

But stuck means there's no WAY out. We know that Jesus is the WAY. In fact, Jesus is the door! There's no way out? Jesus. Jesus is the way out. One day, if you're not there now, you may feel so hopeless and stuck that you won't have any strength to do anything. On that day say, "Jesus. Jesus. Jesus." Keep on saying it. He will make a way. HE IS THE WAY!

He delivered me from my strong enemy and from those who hated and abhorred me, for they were too strong for me. They confronted and came upon me in the day of my calamity, but the Lord was my stay and support. He brought me forth also into a large place ... (Psalm 18:17-19a) God will put your feet in a large place. What you're going through now is just temporary. Don't give up.

No matter how strong the opposition to your marriage is, God in you is stronger. Hold on. Seek God. Act on what He puts in your heart. God has victory and wholeness in mind for your marriage!

17

Getting the Most Out of a Difficult Situation

What if a soldier went into battle KNOWING that the enemy could not defeat her? Not just head knowledge. But heart knowledge, knowing it deep down. She would be strong! She would be able to declare with confidence, "All the power of hell can come against me, but I'm going to win! All the power of hell can come against my marriage and against this ministry, but I AM GOING TO WIN!!! WE are going to WIN!!!" She would be mighty. She would be powerful. She would not be afraid.

That's what you will be like after you go through a time of difficulty and you do not give up! You will emerge out of the struggle as a mighty woman, strong in battle because you realize the enemy cannot defeat you.

Nobody wants to be in a difficult season, but if you're in one, get the most out of it! Here's how.

LET PATIENCE HAVE HER PERFECT WORK

But let patience have her perfect work, that you may be perfect and entire, wanting nothing (James 1:4 KJV). Don't go to the left where you leave God's ways to try to satisfy your flesh, even though it's screaming out to be satisfied. Don't go to the right where you push down your feelings. Stay right in the middle, right under God's thumb. It is the place where you say, "I'm going to do this God's way," at the same time you say, "This hurts, Lord. You know how I feel. Please heal me."

It will definitely feel uncomfortable, but try not to squirm away. God will heal you from things you didn't even know were there. He will change you in ways you didn't know needed changing.

PAY NO ATTENTION

God's love in us is ... *not touchy or fretful or resentful; it takes no account of the evil done to it [it pays no attention to a suffered wrong]* (I Corinthians 13:5). "Pays no attention to a suffered wrong?" you say. "How can that be? *Don't you know what he did to me?* There's no way I can pay no attention to this suffered wrong!"

True, there's no way with man, *but all things are possible with God* (Matthew 19:26b). Notice the Bible says, "God's love in us", not our own weak attempt at love. If you are willing to let go of the world's way of thinking about love—that there is a limit to it, that there are conditions on it, and that after you give a certain amount you don't have to give anymore—then there is space for God to fill you with His love for your husband. I know it hurts and you just want to be loved like you deserve to be, but you're hurting anyway. As soon as you step into God's way of loving, you'll feel better.

Pay no attention to suffered wrongs. This is not to deny you suffered a wrong. Likewise, I'm not telling you the hurt is not there. I am telling you how to have the victory. Yes, you suffered. Of course you need to deal with the issues, but once they're dealt with and you've forgiven those involved, don't go back to the suffering again. Paying no attention to suffered wrongs is a function of the mind. You choose to "pay no attention." How can you do this? It's not as hard as you think.

We tell children to "pay no attention" to someone bothering them. We say, "Ignore them and they'll go away. The person just wants a reaction." We're not telling them the bully is not there. We're telling them how to have the victory. We know that once our kids can pay no attention to a bully, they will have the victory. Once you pay no attention to a suffered wrong, you will have the victory.

The devil serves up old hurts like food. When new hurt comes, even if it's small, the devil serves up old hurts, by saying, "This is just like what happened last time." Eating of it causes you to relive the hurt and produces anger and bitterness. You need to refuse this food. This food comes to you in the form of thoughts. Just say "No!" as soon as the devil tries to bring up an old hurt that's already forgiven. Pay no attention. Set your mind on things above.

I am not trying to—nor could I—give a whole teaching on emotional healing. There are many fine books on emotional healing. Read them. Talk to a counselor. Do whatever it takes to find healing so you can go forward in your marriage. The devil wants to destroy your marriage. God wants to rebuild it. Let God have His way.

BREAK THE GENERATIONAL
CURSE OF DIVORCE

If there is divorce in your family or in your husband's family, you may be suffering from a generational curse of divorce. I was and I had no idea I was.

The generational curse of divorce was this feeling tucked away in the corner of my heart that I was going to end up divorced. I was tormented with thoughts that said, "What makes you think you're so special that you're not going to be divorced?" "Being a Christian is not going to save you! Look at all the Christian people that are divorced!" "Your grandmother was divorced and so was your mother. You're next." "There's no way you can get out of this." It was horrible.

My mother was divorced after eight years of marriage, so when I was married about seven and a half years, I started acting really strange and almost caused my marriage to end. Chris asked, "What is wrong with you? You're acting so strange." I didn't know what was wrong with me and I wasn't able to stop it. What I was doing was preparing for Chris to leave, like my father had. It was completely subconscious!

I thank God that he brought Dr. Roy and Pauline Hawthorne as guest speakers to our church to teach on generational curses. As they were teaching, I realized I had a generational curse of divorce on my life. Right there I said, "In the Name of Jesus, I break the power of this generational curse of divorce over my life." Immediately all the tormenting thoughts stopped and I've never had them again, and I stopped acting strangely. (Well, for the most part!)

If you think you may have a generational curse of divorce or anything else on your life, stop right here and pray this prayer. "Lord, I thank You for the blood of Jesus that covers me and my husband. I thank You for Your Word that says, 'What God hath joined together, let no man put asunder.' I thank You for Your Name that is above every name. Right now, in Jesus' Name, I break the generational curse of divorce that is over my life. Thank You, Lord, that You have set me free. 'He whom the Son sets free is free indeed.'"

DON'T GO BACK

Once God sets you free, refuse to go back to the past. You will need to be aggressive. One night when I was doing the dishes, I was considering something I had done. My thoughts naturally went to, "Oh, I act like that because my parents were divorced."

God had already healed me and set me free from those hurts. He had already broken the power of the generational curse, but I was walking right back into the cage that the devil had waiting for me. I didn't want to go back. I knew I needed to fight.

So right there in the kitchen I said, "In the Name of Jesus, I cut myself off from my past. God has already healed me and I am not controlled by past events." Then I started speaking out who I was in Christ according to the Word of God. "I'm a daughter of the King. I'm seated in heavenly realms with Christ. I am led and controlled by the Holy Spirit." My mind and my spirit were renewed and I had victory.

When God sets you free, make sure you don't put the chains back on! Walk in the freedom and newness of life He gives you. Then you will be able to operate in the strong position in which God has put you.

No one wants to go through an extremely difficult time in her marriage. But if you find yourself in that place, get the most out of it. When the season of difficulty and pain is over, you will be STRONG. You will no longer fear what the devil can do to you. You win. The victory you enjoy can never be taken away from you!

18

What You Need To Know

You are going to do great things. You are going to accomplish much! I believe you will ... *possess the nations and make the desolate cities to be inhabited* (Isaiah 54:3). I believe that ... *great will be your peace and undisturbed composure* ... (Isaiah 54:13). I believe that you will ... *triumph over opposition* ... (Isaiah 54:17).

I pray that God will show you a glimpse of what He has planned for you and your husband to do, all the people that you will affect, all the positive changes that will take place because you are submitting to God's will. I pray that you will believe and not doubt. I pray that you will be courageous and vigorous in your fight and that you won't hold back.

You are going to accomplish much. You don't have time to learn about marriage the long (and hard) way, like I did. The kingdom of God is advancing and He needs whole marriages to lead the way—right now.

The next five chapters cover principles that I wish I knew when I was first married. You need to learn these principles and put them into practice right away. Knowing them will keep you from fighting against God by mistake. Putting them into practice will cause you to get to the place where God wants and needs you to be, quickly.

   ... *spare not; lengthen your cords and strengthen your stakes* (Isaiah 54:2).

19

God Is Your Husband

There is a way of thinking about love that uses the illustration of bank accounts to show how our emotions work. Every time we use our words and actions to love someone, encourage someone, or help someone, we are making a deposit in their emotional bank account. Every time we say something mean or hurtful or act rudely, we are making a withdrawal.

The emotional bank account illustration is a great way to remember how important it is to make deposits in your husband's life. However, if you turn this theory around and use it to gauge how poorly your husband is doing because he has made so many withdrawals from your "account", it can be dangerous. In a difficult time in your marriage you will surely run out of the ability to give love to your husband because you are emotionally depleted yourself. Too many withdrawals have been made from your emotions, leaving you paralyzed and unable to give anymore.

How are you to live then? Love your husband like God loves you—unconditionally. It took me *years* to realize this, because I thought marriage was about me being happy and fulfilled. It's not!

Looking back I see that I would serve my husband and do good things for him just so I could get something back. I would make him a nice dinner and then expect him to sit on the couch with me and hold my hand. Of course, none of this was verbalized, and I wasn't even thinking it consciously, but it was there. When Chris responded liked I'd planned everything was okay, but oh those times when he didn't fit into "the way it was suppose to be"! I would get mad and think he was terrible.

Thank God he freed me from this wrong way of thinking and acting. This was not true love; it wasn't God's love. In fact it was only self-love. I was only concerned about getting my own needs met.

IT STARTS WHEN WE'RE YOUNG

Where did I get my "the way it's suppose to be" set-in-stone ideas from? Where do you get yours from? It starts when we're young. When my daughter, Alyssa, was four years old she was already making plans. "I am going to marry this certain person.... He is going to act like.... We're going to have this many kids.... We're going to take a trip to...." At four years old she had her married life planned! By the time we're adults and we get married, we have our minds set on what our lives are going to be like, what we will do, the way our husbands will treat us— the way it's supposed to be! However, this way of thinking only traps us into selfishness and disappointment.

The world—which promotes the opposite of God's ways— shapes our thinking in this area. Take movies, for instance.

On the one hand there are romantic movies which tell us, "there is man out there who can meet all your needs." The single women are trying to meet him. The married women are trying to make their husbands *become* him!

I watched a romantic comedy the other day that really stirred up my emotions and, to be honest, it took me a little while to be okay with the fact that Chris and I weren't riding off in a horse drawn carriage to live happily ever after. This is because Satan's lies are very subtle. The underlying deception here is that there is something better "out there". That's why women leave their husbands; that's why they have affairs. That's why women feel stuck and settle with being miserable. But all this is a lie. As a believer you have everything you need to be emotionally well and to be able to love your husband unconditionally.

On the other hand are the movies that portray the man as horrible. The woman has to struggle to get away from him and when she does her life is great. What we learn from these movies is that "I don't need a man! I'm going to do this by myself!"

Take it from someone from who tried both of these ways of thinking about her husband. Neither one works. Neither one is right.

A CASE OF THE SHOULD-BE'S

Hope deferred makes the heart sick ... (Proverbs 13:12 NIV).

Everything in my marriage is not always like I think it should be. It's not always like I want it. Sometimes I really wish it were. I work on what I can change, but there are certain things I can't change. Saying, "It *should be* like this or that" or "he *should be* saying this; he *should be* doing that" does no good. In fact, it just makes you sick. It's what I call "coming down with a case of the should-be's."

When we say, "He should be home for dinner," or "He should be more affectionate," we follow a line of thinking that leads us to a dead end. It only makes us focus on what is lacking. While it may be true he should eat dinner with you or be more affectionate, the "should-be's" will make you sick.

I don't see anywhere in the Bible where it says we should put our minds to "should-be's".

Finally, brothers, whatever is true, whatever is noble,
whatever is right, whatever is pure, whatever is lovely,
whatever is admirable—if anything is excellent or praise-
worthy—think about such things (Philippians 4:8 NIV).

Set your minds on things above, not on earthly things
(Colossians 3:2 NIV).

In everything give thanks for this is the will of the
Father in Christ Jesus concerning you
(I Thessalonians 5:18 NIV).

Somehow our should-be's supersede all these instructions. Why? Deep down we think that our marriage relationship exists so that we will be happy and fulfilled. We are angry because we are not getting what we think we deserve!

There is a cure for this sickness. It's found in concentrating on what is good or right in your relationship and in your life. One time when I was sick with the case of the "should-be's," God said to me, "Karen, your marriage is not the only part of your life. Think about all the things that are good in your life and be thankful." I did and it worked!

The best thing to do, just like with any sickness, is to prevent it from happening in the first place. When you feel yourself going down the "should-be" path, stop, turn around, and go another direction. Go God's direction. God's direction is to think about good things and to be thankful for what we have.

Let's not forget about prayer. Put the situation in God's hands. Let him change what needs to be changed. He's much better at it than we are.

That's what Zenaida did. She decided that she had wasted enough time and energy complaining that her husband should be more affectionate. She repented, let go of the "should-be", and put the situation in God's hands. Zenaida had peace. In time, her husband started being more affectionate. God's ways are much greater than ours are!

YOUR HUSBAND IS NOT YOUR FATHER

It is common to hear that if you didn't have a good father figure, you may have trouble relating to men, and especially your husband, in a proper way. Well, sometimes it's a problem if you did have a good father! Maybe you were always "daddy's little girl". If you were cute enough and showed daddy those dimples or gave him "the wink", you would get out of trouble or daddy would make everything better and take care of you. Now you're frustrated because the same tactics are not working with your husband. Your husband is not your daddy! It's time to grow up and be mature in your marriage.

A good marriage doesn't just happen. You have to work at it. *You make a choice to work at it.* You make a choice to keep those vows. You make a choice that nothing will separate you. You make a choice to work things out. Your choices need to stand whether the feelings are there or not.

You made the choice to get engaged. That choice was backed up by a lot of nice feelings. You made the choice to get married. That choice was also backed up by a lot of nice feelings, and— for most of us—a big party with friends and family, pretty dresses, flowers, rings, presents, cake and lots of picture taking!

But things have changed. No one is throwing you a party now that you've been married seven years, three months and two days. Most likely the feelings come and go or maybe the feelings are completely gone. Find some Holy Ghost determination and work at that marriage. Pray. Serve. Give until it hurts and then give some more. You can do it!

The truth is that before we get married we overlook certain annoying behaviors in our spouses. Then when we get married we say, "Oooh! What's that?" We get our little "I'm going to change my husband" kits out. That's not the kind of work I'm talking about. The kind of work I'm talking about is to accept your husband for who he is and to love him unconditionally. (See First Corinthians 13 for how to do this.) Remember, you have little annoying habits too. As you accept and love your husband, you will be free from the "should-be" sickness and have a happy, healthy marriage.

YOUR HEAVENLY HUSBAND

Where you're headed in your marriage is to love your husband unconditionally, and expect nothing in return. The question, then, is how do you get your needs met? As you *agape* love your husband, where do you get your love? You get it from God. This sounds simple, and we all know this is the right answer, but our minds must be constantly renewed in this area.

It always bothers me when people say to single women, "It's all right, honey. God is your husband." It's like they're saying, "Don't worry that you don't have a *real* husband, God will be your husband *for now.*" What does this mean—that we're married to God and then when he gives us an earthly husband, we *divorce God* to marry the man? This is not right. God is every woman's Husband whether she has an earthly husband or not.

It's the same with God being our heavenly Father. We have no problem with calling God our heavenly Father whether we have an earthly father or not. He is, in fact, our heavenly Father, and helps us in ways that our earthly fathers, no matter how wonderful they are, cannot.

In the same way, God is every woman's Husband, whether you have an earthly husband or not. God is your Husband. He is your First Love. He is your Source. He is your Provider. He provides for your physical, mental, and emotional needs. Many times He uses your earthly husband as a vessel to meet your needs, but not always.

We've all experienced times when the money we needed "just comes out of nowhere" and we know it is God's provision. It is the same with everything God gives us, including love.

Love and encouragement may come from a friend (not another man unless he's like a father), your child, or someone at church. It may also come from preaching you hear, your own personal Bible study and prayer time, a teaching tape or a radio or TV broadcast.

Cindy and Dan, both in full time ministry, were going through a particularly hard time in their marriage that few people knew about. Cindy was flooded with cards and phone calls from people she hadn't heard from in years, telling her she was on their minds and that they were praying for her! That was not coincidence. That was God's provision for her emotional needs! God is not limited in the ways He sends love your way. He is a master at supplying your needs. He will take care of you!

WE GET INTO TROUBLE when we expect our earthly husbands to meet all our needs. They are only humans. Even when he's doing 99 things out of 100 "right" your husband will pick up from you that he "failed". He may even withdraw from you and spend his time doing something at which he can "succeed".

To rely on your earthly husband for everything is nothing short of IDOLATRY. You will continue to have problems until you rely on God only. In Isaiah 50:10, God calls out to the one *who reverently fears the Lord, who obeys the voice of his servant, yet who walks in darkness and deep trouble and has no shining splendor [in his heart].* He says, "*Let him rely on, trust in, and be confident in the name of the Lord, and let him lean on and be supported by his God.*" God is able to and will hold you up no matter what the circumstances. However, if you attempt to "*kindle your own fire,*" says verse 11, if you try to do it your own way, "*you shall lie down in grief and in torment.*"

Don't be hard headed like the Israelites in I Samuel 8. They wanted a king like all the other nations. They rejected God as their king. They rejected Him as their Source and Provider. Samuel warned them about the bad things the king would do.

But they persisted. God gave them King Saul. Saul ended up taking their sons, their daughters, and their land, and made them into slaves. The Israelites had rejected God's provision. They tried to kindle their own fire; they laid down in grief and in torment.

You don't have to lie down in grief and torment anymore. You can be free. Change your thinking to line up with the Word of God.

The truth is your husband is a gift from God. Love him and receive love from him, enjoy him, partner with him, but realize God is your Source. God is your Provider. He is your Heavenly Husband. Daily trust Him to meet all your needs, however He chooses. This way you will be able to truly love and serve your earthly husband without expecting anything in return.

TRUE LOVE

First Corinthians 13:7 says that love ... *endures everything [without weakening]*. True love, God's love, does not get depleted. It does not grow less. It does not ebb away. True love endures everything and doesn't weaken. God showed me that I needed to drop my improper use of the emotional bank account illustration. I was concentrating too much on "should-be's" and on what I didn't have. When I threw out my wrong thinking I felt empty, but then I asked God to fill me up with His love. He did. Now not only are my needs are met, but I also have a love for my husband that doesn't weaken.

Make every effort to get to the place where you rely totally on God as your heavenly Husband to meet all your needs and where you love your earthly husband unconditionally. The sooner you can arrive there, the happier you'll be!

Not only will you be happier, but you will also be stronger. The enemy will not be able to control and manipulate you. He will not be able to keep you down, paralyzed by selfish, frustrating, and unproductive thoughts. You will be able to stand strong next to your husband, pray for him, support him, and see the kingdom of God advance!

20

Turning Conflicts
Into Conquests

GOD WILL HAVE HIS WAY IN US. God's purposes will stand. In Isaiah 46:10 the Lord says, "My *counsel shall stand, and I will do all My pleasure and purpose.*" It's what we all pray for. It's what we all desire—that God's purposes will be fulfilled in our lives. We sing, "Have Your way, Lord!" We proclaim, "Whatever it takes!" Then when God starts to work on us, when He digs in there and says, "Okay, this must go," we become indignant and say, "No way!"

Why? I think it's because a lot of times we don't realize that it is God who is doing it.

In order for God's purposes to be accomplished in your life, in order for God to be glorified in your life, self must be out of the way. Your flesh must be crucified. Many times God uses your closest relationship—the relationship with your husband—to accomplish this.

No matter what you are doing in service to the Lord or how much time you spend doing it, God has His eye on you and your husband and wants to advance you. When He advances you, His kingdom advances and you feel fulfilled. To not move into what God has for you is to be miserable. In order for you to move forward into what God has for you, your character must improve. Self must die and your willingness to yield to the Holy Spirit must grow.

SAYING "I DO" MEANS "I DIE TO MYSELF"

Expect God to work on your character and on your husband's character *within* your marriage. Problems in marriage come when people don't realize that this is how it works. They think the marriage exists to meet all of their emotional needs. They don't realize that when they say, "I do," they're really saying, "I die to myself."

When conflicts arise they spend all their time being angry with the other person and trying to figure out how to change the other person. Some people even try to get out of the ministry or get their husbands out because they think the ministry is the cause of their problems.

Leslie was like that. Her husband Brian was a pastor and she hated it. She thought all the problems they had were because of the church. After years of pressing Brian to leave the full-time ministry, he did. He went out and started working a "regular" job. Did the problems go away? No. In fact, they increased. The problem is usually not *in* the ministry. It's in *you*. God wants to set you free. Know that He will use conflicts in your marriage to crucify your flesh so you can be free from its control.

When situations come up between you and your husband that are, let us say, unpleasant, don't get angry with your husband and hate him. Don't concentrate on what he is doing wrong or on how you can change him. Put aside thoughts like, "Why did I ever marry *this* guy?" or "How did I end up with *him*?" (You thought you were the only one who thought that way, didn't you?) Instead, ask God, "What are you trying to do in *me*?"

Recently I asked a woman what she thought God wanted her to do in a certain situation. As she started to answer, her friend jumped in with, "No, she means in a spiritual way, not in a practical way!" I told her, "Spiritual is practical."

God is practical and He wants us to be led be His Spirit in the simplest, most practical situations of every day life. It is there, as you turn some of those conflicts with your husband into conquests over your flesh, that God's purposes will be fulfilled in you and you will walk in the perfect plan God has for you.

Maria liked to listen to teaching tapes while driving in her car. She used to leave the album, with a number of tapes in it, on the front seat of the car so she would always have them ready to pop into the player. But sometimes when she got in the car they wouldn't be where she had left them! They would be *thrown* into the back! She would get so angry. "Why does Mark do that? *He* listens to *his* tapes, but *I* can't listen to *mine*? He has to *throw* them in the back? I hate when he does that," she would fume.

Then one day when she was about to go into her regular rage, she stopped and asked, "God, what are you trying to show me here?" Immediately the verse, *Prefer one another better than yourself* jumped into her head. (God is very quick to answer when we ask Him that question.)

Maria thought, "I know Mark really does not like things to be left in the car. He doesn't like it messy. Furthermore, my tapes are in the way if someone rides in the car with him. Then he has to put the tapes in the back. From now on, I'll carry the tapes with me each time, and if I forget to bring them one time I'll just not listen to them." As Maria went into the house with her tapes, she realized that she was overflowing with peace and joy and she praised and worshiped God. Maria was so thankful that God had corrected her. It set her free.

Every time God corrects us there's a little less of us and a little more of Him in our lives. Then we are free to be whom He made us to be and do what He made us to do! God's purpose stands in our lives.

CORRECTION, NOT REJECTION

Proverbs 3:11 says ... *do not despise or shrink from the chastening of the Lord* .... Sometimes we despise the chastening of the Lord because we think it comes with rejection. While you may have experienced rejection when someone in your past corrected you, it is not so with God. He never rejects you. His chastening is sweet. His correction is always for our good and always brings us righteousness, peace and joy. He is a loving Heavenly Father who just does not like to see us in bondage, so be open to God's correction.

God wants you to be free from everything that will hurt you. Take rebellion, for instance. It will cause you to miss out on God's blessings in every area of your life, so God definitely wants to root it out of you. Marriage is the perfect place to do that.

If conflicts keep coming up where you have a hard time submitting to and adapting to your husband, then stop and ask God, "What are you trying to do here?" I remember one time Chris said, "Don't go to the store now." "*Don't go to the store now?*" I thought. "Yes, I *am* going to the store. I planned *earlier* that I would go to the store *now*. And I *want* to go to the store." My will was having a fit, but somehow through all the protesting, I heard God's still small voice say, "Obey Me! Don't go to the store now!"

Through many instances such as this, the Lord broke me out of rebellion, or rather, broke rebellion out of me. It took longer than it should have taken, but God persevered with me. Now as I submit to the authority God has set in every area of my life— my job, my ministry, my home—I have tremendous success in all these areas and the blessings of God abound in my life. I thank God for His correction. It set me free and caused God's purposes to stand in my life.

EVERY DAY LIFE

A lot of times we look for God to do His work through the big events and big situations in our lives. When we do, we can miss what he is trying to accomplish in everyday "small" situations. God will develop patience in you when you have to wait for your husband longer than you think you should have to. He'll teach you gentleness and kindness when you feel wronged, but requires you to love. You'll experience the blessings of humility when you decide you don't always have to prove you're right.

The truth is that there are a thousand small conflicts in between the big ones. Your response to these conflicts will determine how much God's purposes may be fulfilled in your life and how much God will be glorified through your life. Let God have His way. Let God correct you during these life experiences.

When you do you will find skillful and godly wisdom. Happy [blessed, fortunate, enviable] is the man who finds skillful and godly wisdom ... [drawing it forth from God's Word and life's experiences] (Proverbs 3:13). This wisdom is better than silver, gold and rubies (vs. 14-15); it is a highway of pleasantness (vs. 17), and a tree of life (vs. 18). Wow! That would be enough right there, but the scripture goes on to say this wisdom you receive from allowing God to correct you is ... life to your inner self, and a gracious ornament to your neck (your outer self) (vs. 22).

Life to your inner self is so important because you're the only person you can never get away from. You can get away from other people if they are depressing, negative and full of death, but you can't get away from yourself when there is death in your inner self! Make it a point to get wisdom from everyday conflicts in your marriage and you will receive life.

This life can then be passed on to your husband, your marriage, your children, and everyone you minister to. You will be standing strong in and operating powerfully from the position in which God has placed you!

21

A Step Farther

Just when you think you've got something down, God digs in again and shows you more junk in your life and requires you to let go of it. It's like there are layers of wrong attitudes and sin and He just keeps on peeling them away. But praise God! It's always for our good.

I had been practicing dying to self in the small conflicts as I talked about in the last chapter, but then a big conflict came along. What I learned changed my whole outlook on problems and dying to self.

Chris made me really angry one day. I can't remember the issue, but I'm sure it was entirely his fault. (*Just kidding!*) All I wanted to do is get out of the house. I had to get away. I was going to go away for a couple of days, but then I decided, "No, I'll just stay out really late so he'll know I am angry and maybe he'll worry about me." So I went to the bank to get out money to go to the mall.

By the time I finished at the bank, I had calmed down enough to hear God saying to me, "You not listening to Me about this. You need to consult Me." God knew that by this time in my life I was determined to obey Him quickly and completely. Not really wanting to know what He would say, I tried to appease God with, "Okay, here's the revised plan. I'm going to the mall and staying out late, but I'll call Chris and tell him in a *really nice voice* what my plans are so he won't worry." I was hoping to get to hold on to my anger.

God was neither impressed nor satisfied. He said, "Go home and make Chris dinner." "Go home and make Chris dinner? No way! That's the last thing I want to do!" I thought, "Maybe I missed God" and tried to offer Him one of my alternate plans again. But there it was again as clear as a bell. "Go home and make Chris dinner." Then He added, "You can do what you want, but know if you do, then it won't be My best." Ugh!

I was really stuck. My flesh was raging. My spirit wanted to obey God. It was as if my flesh and my spirit were in a wrestling match, fighting it out, and neither one was winning.

Then help came from somewhere. In the corner of my mind I started thinking about the verse "Narrow is the path that leads to life." (Thank you, Holy Spirit.) I saw myself on a narrow path. I was at a point on the path where there was a side of a mountain on one side and a huge rock on the other. I could just barely squeeze through—but only if I left most of my "self" behind. No extra baggage. No attitudes and "rights" that I thought were a permanent part of me could go along.

"Narrow is the path that leads to life...*Narrow* is the path that *leads to life*. Wait a minute," I thought. "*This narrow path leads to life.* So actually leaving my 'self' behind *leads to life*. Dying to self *leads to life*."

It was a huge realization for me. I had always thought of dying to self as this horrible thing that you just had to do, but sitting in my car on Myrtle Avenue on a Saturday afternoon, I realized that dying to self was the best thing I could do for myself. Dying to self actually benefits you! So I laid down my anger and submitted my will to God. I went home and made Chris dinner. We had a great evening and I had peace! (The longer you're married, the more you treasure it.) I found life that day.

In Deuteronomy 30:19 NIV Moses tells the Israelites, "I have set before you life and death.... Now choose life so that you and your children may live." Choose to die to self, to die to the flesh in all situations. It's actually choosing life and the best thing you can do for yourself!

THE MARTYR SYNDROME

Although we now see that dying to self is wonderful, we have to be careful of the martyr syndrome. The martyr syndrome is where you put down your feelings for the sake of others, but at the same time you hold onto bitterness and anger. This is not dying to self. This is faking it and letting self hold onto something.

The martyr syndrome is easy to fall into when you and your husband are minister to others. Beware of it! It has the potential to kill you.

In difficult circumstances you will always be tempted to go for this fake dying to self. I was tempted to on that day I described above. Not being ignorant of the schemes of the devil, I knew the devil would love for me to flip out on a Saturday. Then it would affect Chris negatively and in turn it would affect the whole church because he had to preach the next day. Part of my thinking was, "Maybe I should calm down for the sake of the church," but I couldn't do it just for the sake of the church even though I love the people and want the best for them. I knew I was still holding on to anger. I had to deal with it.

I have seen other women sacrifice themselves for the sake of others, but hold on to hurt, anger and bitterness while doing it. I don't think they meant to; nevertheless they did. They just tucked their negative feelings away in the hidden corners of their souls. It worked for a while, but then after all the "corners" were filled to overflowing, the negative feelings had to come out. When they did, they came out violently.

This is why pastors' wives have nervous breakdowns. This is why they "suddenly" run away from their husbands and families and churches and say, "It's time to take care of me!" They go crazy and you never hear from them again. I don't want to go crazy. I just want to serve God.

I decided to tell God how I felt. I told Him I really wanted to obey Him. I really wanted to show love to Chris, and I really wanted the congregation to have the best, but I had this anger and was unable to get rid of it myself. I felt like I was showing God a huge open wound, but He didn't look away or turn away. He wasn't disgusted. I told Him, "I don't want this anymore."

I didn't feel happy, but I did feel peace. Then a desire to worship Him came over me. I worshiped. I don't know what happened to the anger. It just went away and it is has never come back. It's not hidden or tucked away, waiting to explode like a time bomb. Thank God!

Beware of the martyr syndrome. If the devil can't destroy you today, he'll do it the "slow cooker" way and wreak havoc in your life and in all those around you ten years from now. As a woman who sincerely wants the best for everyone, you are a huge candidate for this kind of destruction.

YOU HAVE THREE CHOICES

The question is not whether or not you will experience hurt and pain. Hurt and pain are a part of life. The question is what you will do with the hurt and pain. There are three choices of how to handle it.

> **#1 Follow your flesh.** Indulge in anger, bitterness, and fear. Hold onto it and don't let it go. Do your own thing. Find your own satisfaction if nobody's going to give it to you. Problem: The flesh doesn't satisfy.

#2 Convince yourself it doesn't matter. Ignore your feelings. Problem: The negative feelings do not go away and will surface later.

#3 Open up to God and say, "I'm hurting. This is painful. Please help me." Listen for and obey His instructions. Receive His love and mercy and help.

Choice #3 is obviously the only good choice. Please don't try the other two! God wants to help you.

The Bible teaches that the Lord is your healer. It doesn't say "your husband is your healer." If your husband or someone else hurts you, know that they will not be able to heal you. Only God can heal you. Likewise, when you hurt your husband or other people, you cannot heal them. Only God can. Call out to God for help. *Heal me, O Lord, and I shall be healed; save me, and I shall be saved, for You are my praise* (Jeremiah 17:14). The Lord is your healer!

Lisa's husband Doug was going through a mid-life crisis. Nothing satisfied him, including her. He withdrew from Lisa physically and emotionally. It became so bad that they eventually separated. During this time Lisa experienced a lot of hurt. When Doug realized what he had done and that he really did want to be with Lisa, he came back to her, wanting to work things out.

Lisa wanted to get back together, but it was hard for her. She mistakenly thought that since Doug did things to hurt her, he needed to do things to heal her. But no matter what he did, she still felt wounded. It was only when she cried out to God for help that she was healed of all her hurts and was able to go on in victory.

Tell God when you feel uncomfortable. He will help you. About every other month Tenisha, whose husband Marcos is the senior pastor at their church, doesn't even feel like going to church. At the same time she feels obligated to and deep down inside really wants to. She's tempted to just go and fake it, to plaster a smile on her face and shake hands and "kiss babies," all the while hating it on the inside. Tenisha realizes this is dangerous. She stops those negative thoughts and goes to God with them. "When I'm honest with Him," she says, "He always fixes the problem in me. I don't really know how. I just feel better." Tenisha is smart. She's determined not to let herself get caught in a trap.

Be determined not to get caught in a trap either. When you start to feel the "squeeze", stop and ask God for help. Ask Him for understanding. Don't follow after the flesh or try to figure it out with your carnal mind.

Romans 8:6 says *Now the mind of the flesh [which is sense and reason without the Holy Spirit] is death.* If you try to figure it out without the help of the Holy Spirit, the devil can easily slip ideas into your mind that aren't true. He'll say, "This is just the way it is," and "You just have to suck it up." These lies may give temporary solutions, but again, over the years all the stuff you "sucked up" for the sake of other people is inside you and it's going to come out and damage or destroy you and many of those around you.

Safeguard yourself. Don't stop short in your thinking. Make sure you're not holding onto any negative emotions. Be honest with God. Take it all the way through to peace.

The only way to go forward with God is to keep traveling that narrow path. There will be times between you feel like you have to pass between a rock and the side of a mountain. Just let go of what you have to let go of and keep going forward. God has life for you.

When you receive life from God, you can give it to others. I know that's your heart's desire!

22

Enjoying Your Marriage

Enjoy your life. Enjoy your marriage. Don't wait until everything is perfect. You'll miss out on life! As you and your husband are accomplishing great things for God, you're supposed to be enjoying it!

Enjoying is a mindset. You *make up your mind* to enjoy something or someone. Each strength your husband has is accompanied by a weakness. *Make up your mind* to enjoy the strengths.

Enjoy your husband's personality. What drew you to him in the first place? Think about it. Take a minute and write it down. It will help you.

Did you write it down? Go do it. I'll wait....

Were you surprised by what you wrote? Kathy was when she did this exercise. She realized that one of the things that drew her to her husband was that he was hard to get close to. She found it challenging and exciting to get close to him. Thinking back on this made her realize that she can't complain now when she finds it hard to communicate with him! Kathy actually enjoys "the challenge" once again!

Madelyn had difficult relationships with men before she met Christ. She didn't want to be hurt any more and decided she and her three children would just have to make it on their own. Then God brought this wonderful, kind, loving man, Bill, into her life. His careful attention and doting was just what she needed. After a few years, though, it began to annoy her.

When Madelyn took the "remember what you liked about your husband" test, she realized she needed to stop fretting over her husband being "overly loving". Now when her husband displays his undying love, Madelyn doesn't feel overwhelmed. She enjoys this characteristic of her husband once again.

What you liked about your husband before you were married may be annoying to you now. But you can make up your mind to enjoy this part of your husband's personality again. Or maybe you just forgot what you liked about him. Keeping it in the fore-front of your mind will help you enjoy him!

BE PREMATURELY NOSTALGIC

Nostalgia is a bittersweet longing for the past. "Those were the days!" we exclaim. Was everything about "those days" great? No, but we remember them as great. In our marriages we need to be *prematurely nostalgic*. We need to have a "bittersweet longing for the old days," today, as we are living the "old days".

Your marriage will go through different seasons. Most of these seasons happen only once. You can't go back. There is good and bad in each season, so just enjoy it for what it is.

You will look back and say that some of the rough times were also some of the best, so why not say it now and enjoy them? Say, "I love these rough times! They are making us strong."

Rejoice now! *Shouts of joy and victory resound in the tents of the righteous* ... (Psalm 118:15 NIV). I used to think it said, "Shouts of joy and victory *will* resound in the tents of the righteous". I thought it meant that if you stay with the program, if you keep on doing what is right, if you struggle through, then one day you would rejoice. It doesn't. It's not written in the future tense.

It's written in the present tense.

Shouts of joy and victory resound in the tents of the righteous *right now*. Shouts of joy and victory resound in the tents of the righteous *regardless of your circumstances!* When you go through a difficult time in your marriage or in your ministry, go around your house shouting for joy and praising God.

This joy in the midst of difficulty is spiritual warfare. Your rejoicing throws the devil off. He doesn't know what to do with you! *Let the high praises of God be in their throats and a two-edged sword in their hands* (Psalm 149:6).

Don't wait until later to rejoice. Rejoice now! And rejoice later when things improve. *Rejoice in the Lord always and again I say, "Rejoice!"* (Philippians 4:4 KJV)

YOUR MARRIAGE IS UNIQUE

You are unique. There is nobody exactly like you. The life that God has set before you is unique. In Hebrews 12:1, the life that God has set before you is compared to a race. *... and let us run with patient endurance and steady and active persistence the appointed course of the race that is set before us.*

We know that because God has set before each of us an individual race we do not compare ourselves to each other. We pursue God and who He has for us to be and what He has for us to do.

It is the same thing for your marriage. You are unique. Your husband is unique.

unique you + unique husband = unique marriage

Your marriage is unique. Enjoy it for what it is. Just like you can't compare your life to somebody else's, you can't compare your marriage to somebody else's.

In addition, don't try to make your marriage like somebody

else's. You will become frustrated and disappointed.

Maybe you grew up admiring someone's marriage. Maybe it was your parents' marriage, your pastor's marriage, or a close friend's. That's great, but now that you're married, don't try to make your marriage exactly like theirs. Learn from these good marriages, but don't try to squish your marriage into some mold. It won't work and you will be disappointed and your husband will be annoyed!

Be yourself. Let your husband be himself. The truth is that there are several aspects of good relationships. Some couples talk to each other a lot about their feelings. Some work together well. Some couples hold hands walking down the street. Some couples are strong. Your relationship will have some of these characteristics, but not all of them.

I'll never forget the time I told Chris that I wanted to be more like this couple we knew from another ministry. They looked so cute and they would hold hands and everything seemed perfect. Chris just looked at me and said, "Karen, they just started counseling because it just came out that he was having an affair." Needless to say, that was the last time I wanted my marriage to be like somebody else's!

Perhaps you have thoughts lingering in the back of your mind like, "We must be doing something wrong. This is not right. We don't do devotions together like other couples do. We don't pray together like I heard we should." Well, struggle no more.

Women are both shocked and relieved when I tell them Chris and I don't have family devotions and we don't pray together. Do I think family devotions are bad? Of course not! If you sit down and study the Bible and pray with your husband, enjoy it and make the most of it. I'm just saying it's not something we do and I don't feel guilty about it or try to make it happen. We do have great discussions about God and about what we are learning, but we don't have a set time for those discussions to take place.

Don't put yourself in a box. Look at nature! God is the King of variety! The roses don't try to be like the sunflowers and the eagles don't try to be like the sparrows. They concentrate on who they are and who God made them to be and the world is beautiful. Enjoy your unique marriage! It's different than everybody else's!

Jennifer would get upset every time she and her husband Robert were around Julia and Phil. Phil would always open the car door for Julia and carry all her packages. Jennifer desperately tried to get Robert to do the same. She thought something must be wrong in their marriage because he wouldn't do it. Finally, Jennifer stopped comparing her marriage to Julia's. She concentrated on what was good about her marriage and found peace and happiness.

ENJOY YOUR DIFFERENCES

I must admit that for the first several years of our marriage, I enjoyed the similarities Chris and I had, while I ignored the differences. Chris was such a godly man who wanted a totally adventurous life on the edge, serving God. He cared more about helping people than how or where he lived. I liked that. We were the same.

Whenever any differences came up, I didn't pay much attention to them. I just shrugged them off and went on. This worked well for several years. Then at some point, I don't know exactly when, it seemed there were more differences than similarities. As the differences became more profound, I desperately tried to shove them into the corner and live like I had always lived. The situation only became worse.

I couldn't/didn't enjoy Chris that much anymore and I felt like he didn't enjoy me. I felt as if I was on down hill skis and my legs were getting farther and farther apart. You know that's not a good situation to be in!

What's more is that this was happening as Chris and I were both pressing in and seeking God. That didn't make sense to me. "One of us must be missing God," I thought, "and I don't think it's me!" The differences were taking over and they would have killed our marriage if I hadn't learned what I am telling you here today. Enjoy your differences!

It's actually very simple to do. When a difference comes up don't say, "Oooh, why does he have to be like that?" Instead, say, "I enjoy our differences. I enjoy our differences. I enjoy our differences," and then you will.

This has freed me up so much and I believe it has caused me to be more enjoyable to be with. Now I am absolutely thrilled with our differences! He is so much of what I am not and I need that.

There are two reasons it took me so long to gain victory in this area. The first reason is that I wasn't expecting it. I thought that what worked in the beginning would be the way it always worked, but that's not true. God keeps on growing us, changing us, and improving us and we have to flow with the changes.

The second reason was fear. I thought that it was our similarities that kept us together. Therefore, our differences must break us apart. I didn't want to be broken apart, so I resisted the differences. It was incorrect thinking.

Don't let either of those reasons keep you from enjoying your husband to the fullest. Enjoy your unique similarities *and* your unique differences!

YOUR MARRIAGE HAS
UNIQUE CHARACTERISTICS

Seek God. Ask Him what the characteristics of your marriage are. Ask Him to show you the purpose of your marriage.

My marriage is characterized by strength. Chris and I are both moving forward and pushing forward. Both of us are pursuing

God. So our marriage is strong and moving. Chris inspires me. I see his faithfulness, his determination, his perseverance. This man never gives up! He pursues God with fervor! That motivates me to be the same way. We spur each other on to good deeds, not by telling each other, but by living out our lives in front of each other.

Our marriage is also characterized by struggle. In order for Chris to get up and preach and bring words of life to struggling people it has to be. He has to understand what they feel. In order to encourage and motivate other ministers like he does, Chris must go through many struggles himself.

Over the years we've opened our home to several foster children. Talk about struggle! I'll never forget the early years when we were having trouble with two boys we had taken in. They were very insecure. One would get angry when I gave the other one attention. They were so angry. They took it out on anyone in their path. One day they even threw rocks at me and cursed at me. I was frustrated, upset, and crying because everything wasn't working out like I thought it would. Chris sat me down and said, "Karen, we are not going to have a cute little family."

God has said the same thing to me about my marriage. "Karen, you're not going to have a cute little marriage." Victorious? Yes! But with struggle. That's just the way it is. I have to struggle so I can speak into your life. I'm willing to do that. Actually, I don't have much of a choice. (The Potter. The clay. "How can you say, 'What are you making?'" But that's the subject of a whole other book!)

Maybe you struggle in your marriage too. Maybe not. Ask God to give you insight into your marriage. Then you can move forward strongly and you can stop trying to make it into what it will never be. Now that's freedom. This new freedom will cut down on the striving.

In fact, make every effort to stop striving. The striving comes because you desire something outside the grace given you. God gives you the grace and ability to be who you're suppose to be, not for who you are trying to be outside of His will. Don't fight against God.

BE OPEN TO CHANGE

Now that I've made a case for accepting your marriage for what it is, know this: Just like an individual changes and improves, so will your marriage. You are not stuck in a box. In fact, although my marriage has had many struggles, it is now moving into a real time of joy! So look for and receive those changes as God brings them.

Enjoy who you are. Enjoy who you husband is. Relax. Let God design you, form you, and make you what you ought to be.

First Timothy 6:17 NIV says that God *richly provides us with everything for our enjoyment.* So enjoy now as you advance the Kingdom of God! Don't wait until later!

23

Don't Believe the Lies

See to it that no one takes you captive through hollow and deceptive philosophy, which depends on human tradition and the basic principles of this world, rather than on Christ.
—Colossians 2:8 NIV

I was sitting in a hotel room reading a book about family relationships. The book was explaining that children of divorce have little hope of experiencing a good family life when they're adults. It went on to say that children who are abused are *really* messed up, especially if they are sexually abused.

It seemed all the things the book talked about happened to me as I was growing up. I believed what it was saying about my chances as an adult. I ended up on a heap on the hotel floor crying, "That means there's no hope! That means my family will be crazy! That means I won't be able to help anyone! That means I'm going to have a horrible life! I AM SO DYSFUNC-TIONAL!"

What was happening? I was being taken captive through hollow and deceptive philosophy that depended on the basic principles of this world. I was leaving no room for Christ and God's healing power!

I was so upset that it took me until the next day to calm down enough to hear God tell me, "I'm greater than that. You certainly will have a great life. You certainly will be free."

The same thing can happen with personality tests. "I'm a QZET!" "See this chart, that's me." "Well, I'm melancholy. I think deeply. I'm serious. I'll really never be able to enjoy life." While these tests are wonderful for understanding yourself and others, you can also get trapped in them because they, by themselves, leave no room for Christ. Please understand, I'm not faulting the tests; they can be a reliable source of information. The problem occurs when people allow themselves to be taken captive by the findings and don't rely on Christ.

LET'S NOT BE IGNORANT

Since the devil cannot take you out of the strong position God has put you in, he tries to convince you to step down from it. When you base your thinking on the principles of the world and not on Christ, you step down from your strong position to walk in agreement with the enemy, instead of walking in agreement with God.

Therefore, worldly philosophies and mindsets are dangerous. They cripple you. You're not able to stand and fight, or fulfill your purpose as you ought to.

Maybe you didn't realize you had any worldly mindsets. That is the devil's plan. He's been hiding in the shadows, laughing at you as you agree with him. Remember this is a war and the devil does not play fair. You are a target. Because your mind is a seat of power in your life, your mind is a target.

Following are just a few of the worldly mindsets I have seen in myself and in others. Feel free to add your own to the list as the Lord reveals them to you.

You can't have a close friend because your husband is a minister.

Lie! Lie #312. (We should just number them. He uses the same ones over and over on all of us!) While you need to be careful whom you confide in, God will certainly give you a friend if you ask Him for one. He is big enough. Trust Him to do it.

You can't be yourself. You have to be who everyone expects you to be.

Chris and I were in full-time ministry at *Metro* several years before he started pastoring the adult congregation. When he stepped into that position, I just kept on doing what I had always done. One of those things was to drive the bus to bring people to church for the Sunday morning service.

One day a dear older woman was shocked to see me driving the bus. She exclaimed, "The pastor's wife should not be driving a bus!" "I really enjoy driving the bus," I answered with a smile. "To me, there's nothing better than bringing people to church so they can hear about Jesus." "Oh" was her only audible response, but I could see the wheels turning in her head.

Within a few weeks she was involved in the Sidewalk Sunday School that meets near the building where she lives. Then she started to help visit all the children in her neighborhood. Now she is the lay pastor for the whole area and is making a way for many to hear about Jesus every week.

Do I think I am the sole reason for this? No, but it couldn't have hurt! Praise God we are allowed to be ourselves.

There is a certain "wife of a man in the ministry" mold you have to fit into.

Closely related to the one above, this mindset is about what you expect from yourself. In other words, you're comparing yourself to another wife of a man in the ministry and coming up short.

Debbie was concerned because she and Mike didn't have any kids. All the pastors she ever had were parents. She thought she and Mike could not be good pastors unless they had kids.

Don't try to be exactly like someone you know even if she is admirable. You are not that other person. God does not need two of that other person. You are you. Seek God. Let Him make you into whom you need to be.

If you are thinking you have to be someone other than your-self, someone everyone expects you to be, or more like the last woman who was in your position, realize it's a trap! Don't fall into it. If you're already in the trap, get out of it. (More on that below.)

The ministry is horrible because you live in a "glass house".

Evelyn, whose husband was just ordained and was planting a new church, went out with some of the area pastors' wives to find out what it was like to be married to a minister. Hoping for some encouragement, as she was a little nervous about the whole venture, she was deeply disappointed. The pastors' wives had nothing good to say, but, rather, told her how horrible the ministry is because you live in a "glass house" and everyone is always looking at you. That's so sad because they are believing a lie!

It's true that people look at you, but it's a lie from the devil that it's horrible! On the contrary, it's wonderful. I want people to look at me. I want them to look at me and see me having trouble with my kids. Who are they going to see? A weak me and a big strong Jesus. I want people to know Chris and I don't have it all together. Who are they going to see? A human man and woman and a superhuman Jesus! What are we here for anyway? To show forth God's glory. Let them look!

The wife of a minister in Italy asked me, "Isn't it hard when people look at you?" "It's not hard," I answered, "It's just a greater opportunity to show them Jesus." The truth is this: *God would not put you in that position without giving you the grace to be able to handle it.* I count this position as a privilege. I have more influence on people than I did before.

This is it. It won't get any better than this.

Sometimes you experience a great time of growth and you think, "God has already given me so much. There can't be any more. I better just be thankful." This is especially true as you get older and think, "God has allowed me to do so much. This is it."

Even though you have a desire for more, the devil lies to you and tells you this holy desire is just selfish ambition. The truth is that God is longing to be gracious to you (Isaiah 30:18), He is a Teacher ever before you (Isaiah 30:20), and you will keep on growing and developing and go from glory to glory.

You can't have a successful ministry and a successful marriage and family.

"If we could just get out of the ministry," some women say, "everything would be okay." "If we could just stop being so involved in the church, everything would be better." That's not true.

Recognize that the devil is trying to squash your ministry by making you think it is the cause of the problems in your marriage and your life. He is trying to get you to hate the work of the Lord by making you think it is stealing your husband. It's just not true. If your husband weren't serving the Lord, you would still have those problems. In fact, they might even be worse.

The ministry is not the problem. The problem is your relationship. You need to work it out. Pray it out. Don't let the devil deceive you that it is the ministry's fault!

Don't be like some women I've seen who forced their husbands out of the ministry. They nagged them out of preaching or pastoring or leading and they end up working in a parking garage or at a department store. If your husband is supposed to be working in a parking garage or a department store, then that's fine. But if he is supposed to be preaching, then don't stop him. Find another way to fix your relationship. Try unconditional love and dying to self. No one said it would be easy!

"Look at this hard time you're having! All that praying did NO GOOD!"

This lie is for those of us who have responded to the battle cry and are committed to praying for our husbands. I was giving in to those thoughts one time when suddenly I realized, "If this is how difficult things are and I've been praying, imagine how difficult it would be if I hadn't been praying! Thank God I've been praying!"

RECOGNIZING THE LIE

How do you recognize a human philosophy, a wrong mindset, a lie?

First of all, call on the Holy Spirit. John 16:13 NIV says the Holy Spirit *will guide you into all truth.* Ephesians 5:13 NIV says that *everything exposed by the light becomes visible.* When God shines His light on your heart and mind, the lies are exposed. Ask God to reveal any wrong mindsets you have. Ask Him to shine His light and expose the lies you believe.

The second step is to think about what you are thinking about. Take note, for example, if you are always thinking, "I'm just not as good as that pastor's wife. She does everything better than I do. I wish I could be just like her."

Next, compare what you're always thinking about to the truth. If what you are thinking does not match the truth in God's Word, then you know you are believing a lie. In this example you would say, "God's Word says that I am created in

Christ Jesus to do good works prepared in advance for *me* to do. I do not have to be like anyone else. God strengthens me and makes me able. What I have been thinking is a lie."

It's important to realize that it's not just one, isolated, incorrect thought you're having. It is a mindset, a stronghold, where a lot of wrong thoughts originate. You must get rid of the mindset to be free from the grip of the lies.

GETTING RID OF THE MINDSET

In order to get rid of these ungodly mindsets and wrong thinking patterns, you must consciously reject the lie and receive the truth. It'll take a little bit of a fight, especially if you've had this mindset for a long time.

Let's say the mindset you have is that you must fit into a certain mold because you are a pastor's wife. Very simply you say,

- I reject the way of thinking that says I have to fit into a certain mold because I am a pastor's wife.

- It's not true.

- The truth is that I am God's workmanship, created in Christ Jesus to do good deeds, prepared in advance for me to do. (Ephesians 2:10) The truth is that I can do all things through Christ who strengthens me. I am ready for anything and equal to anything through Him who infuses me with inner strength. (Philippians 4:13) Furthermore, God leads the humble in what is right (Psalm 25:9) and He teaches those who reverently fear Him the way they should choose. (Psalm 25:12) God has specific works for me to do, He makes me able to do them and He will teach me and lead me into what He wants me to do.

- I receive this truth into my life.

Then repeat the truth in different ways until the mindset is totally broken. One way is to thank God. "Thank You that you don't want me to be like anyone else. You have created me to do certain good deeds. They are already prepared and I just have to go do them. Thank You that You strengthen me and I am equal to any task through You." Other ways of repeating the truth are to speak it out to yourself throughout the day and to speak it out to others as much as you can.

At first, you may still walk down the path that wrong thought is leading you. That's okay. This is a process. As soon as you realize it, back up, say "No, thank you," and start down the path of truth. Soon the stronghold will be demolished and those wrong thoughts won't bother you anymore.

Once you see how this works, you'll love it. You will turn in all your wrong mindsets for the truth of God's Word. You will stay strong in your position to fight for your marriage and ministry because you are walking in agreement with God.

Note: *For more on mindsets and wrong thinking patterns, read* **The Battlefield of the Mind** *by Joyce Meyer (Harrison House, Inc. 1995).*

24

Train the Younger Women

*Likewise, teach the older women to be reverent in the way
they live, not to be slanderers or addicted to much wine, but
to teach what is good. Then they can train the younger
women to love their husbands and children, to be self-
controlled and pure, to be busy at home, and to be subject to
their husbands so no one will malign the word of God.*
—Titus 2:3,4 NIV

Maybe you read this book and thought, "I know this stuff. Yep. I've been through that. Uh-huh. I had to learn *that* the hard way." If that's true then please help some younger women. Please help some women who have been married fewer years than you have so they don't have to learn the hard way or end up divorced.

Different generations of women used to spend time together—in quilting circles, or maybe while cooking and canning. Living with or near your extended family was the norm. Older women were there to teach the younger women and there was a time and a place for it to happen. Training and mentoring happened naturally.

Now with our highly mobile society many younger women are not connected with the older women in their families. Add to that the fact that so many women are working outside the home and everyone has separate schedules. Older women training younger women doesn't happen very often, but it needs to.

Think back to when you first got married. What do you know now that you wish you knew then? Think of all the striving and heartache that could have been avoided if you knew what you know now. Think of all the time that you wasted being angry and hurt instead of being peaceful and happy. Wouldn't it have been wonderful if someone had come alongside of you and helped you?

Maybe you did have someone to help you. Maybe you didn't. Regardless, you can be that special person for a young woman or group of women now. You can share with them what you know and help them succeed in marriage and avoid a lot of heartache at the same time.

SHOWING THE WAY

Have you ever been in a line of cars trying to drive by a double-parked truck? The first car goes really slow and it is difficult. The driver doesn't know if she will make it or not. But then when she successfully passes the truck, everyone behind her has an easier time because they saw someone else do it. They saw what she did and how she did it and they can copy what worked. Mentoring younger women is the same thing. It is showing them the best way to go.

If you are unsure of whether you could mentor a younger woman or not, think of a married woman who you admired when you were young. It has to be someone you were able to have personal contact with, not someone from afar on TV.

Now imagine if that woman approached you and said she sees great potential in you and your husband and wants to spend time with you to encourage you in your marriage. How would you feel? You would feel great, encouraged, uplifted! There are probably young women out there who admire you and your marriage. They would love if you would invest in them.

Studies show that people excel at a faster rate when someone believes in them and tells them so. You can make a big difference in a young woman's life!

IT COULD BE YOU!

The older women must train the younger women. Maybe you don't think of yourself as old. I didn't either, but as I felt the burden for the younger married women on our church staff to be helped, I looked around for the older women to teach them. Suddenly, I realized *I* was the older woman to teach them even though I was in my early thirties.

The key is that you are old*er*, not old! You may not even be older in age, but if you are older in the number of years married, you probably have something to offer.

You may think, "I'd be glad to do it if someone asked me," but they probably won't ask you. Either they think you'll say, "No," or they don't even know *to* ask. When you're young you don't know that you don't know. Not only do you not know the answers, you don't even know the questions!

It's up to you to approach the younger woman. Ask God and He will show you whom to talk to. Let her know you see great potential in her and her husband. Tell her that you would like to come alongside her and see her have success in her marriage and all that God has for her life.

Then set up a regular time to meet. Meet for lunch or during the Sunday School class hour. It can be monthly or every couple weeks. The point is to have a specific time with a specific goal.

WHAT TO TALK ABOUT

What do you talk about when you meet with a younger woman or women? Talk about the issues brought up in this book or your own experiences. If you're meeting one on one, then you may ask her what she'd like to talk about. Always have something ready, though, since she won't always know what she doesn't know.

Be aware of what the women are struggling with. For instance, if you notice a young woman talking badly about her husband, teach about the words of our mouths at the next meeting. If a movie comes out with a strong feminist bent, talk about how the world's ways differ from God's ways.

During the first meeting we had at Metro Ministries for all the wives on staff, we talked about the importance of praying for our husbands. I gave a copy of *The Power of the Praying Wife* to everybody. I know another woman who started her group the same way.

A lot of what you talk about will be preventative. The women may not be having problems in a certain area, but you talking about it will either help them when that problem does come up or help them to avoid it altogether. Leading a group will certainly make all your struggles a little more "worth it"!

ONE EXAMPLE

Every month at *Metro Ministries* the staff wives come together at my house for the lunch hour. Everyone is busy and doesn't need an extra meeting to go to, especially one that would take them away from their families. But everyone does need to eat, so we meet for lunch.

We eat and fellowship for the first half hour. Then I or one of the other "older" women gives a short (two or three minute) exhortation on prayer, followed by a ten-minute talk on a certain subject. The remaining time is for group discussion.

It sounds simple and it is. And the results have been great! First of all, as God's ways have been taught and we have come into line with His commands, we are helped, blessed, and our marriages are stronger.

Secondly, meeting once a month has opened up communication among the wives outside the meeting. When the women found out they're not the only ones with a certain problem and that it's okay to admit you're struggling, many good friendships formed and all of us are finding help in a really natural way. There's no more faking it and acting like everything's okay when it's not.

The third great result is in what has *not* happened since we started these meetings. There have been no big "explosions" in any of the staff marriages. How many times have we heard of ministers' marriages "suddenly" falling apart and they are taken right out of the ministry and damage is done to the congregation? Since we've had these meetings, nothing like that has happened.

Our hour together is not a gossip session or a "let me tell you how bad *my* husband is" session. Knowing we are not naturally above this, I made it a matter of prayer from the beginning. Then I led by example. I made sure I never said anything bad about Chris, but talked about struggles I had with myself and the ways I needed to improve. Everyone else followed and not one ill word has been spoken about a man in our meetings. Truly, that would defeat the whole purpose!

One other thing about our meetings is that they are only open to the staff, not all the women in the church. Most of the congregation doesn't even know about it. The reason for this is that I wanted the staff women to have time to be ministered to.

I knew that once someone from congregation came, the staff would immediately go into the roll of serving the congregation. (*Metro* has a wonderful staff!) I believe that if the staff marriages are strong, all the marriages in the church will be positively affected. That is exactly what has happened.

A pastor's wife who visited here from Mexico was glad to hear that. She had a burden to meet with the wives of their church's staff, even though it was only three women. She was feeling guilty about not including the wives in the congregation. When she heard that's how we do it, she knew that's what she needed to do. It confirmed the burden God had given her.

YOUR BURDEN

Maybe your burden will be for the church staff wives, maybe it will be the wives in the congregation or in the particular area you work in. Maybe your burden will be for a woman at work, or maybe it will be for not-yet-saved wives. I figure that if we all ask God for His burden and then act on it, everyone will be covered!

If you would like to have a group like this in your church, but you feel too young or inexperienced, pray and ask God to give you a leader. Give a copy of this book to that person and ask her to consider teaching you.

KNOW WHAT'S COMING

Expect resistance from the enemy. Teaching a woman how to take her strong position as a wife is the last thing he wants you to do.

I've been in the ministry for several years, working out on the streets with children and families in the ghettoes of New York City, seeing many lives changed for the glory of God. NEVER have I felt so much spiritual pressure as I do when I meet with the staff wives of *Metro*. It wasn't until someone started to intercede for me specifically in this area that I felt the pressure subside. Know that when you step out and deliberately teach a younger woman how to succeed in her marriage and how to be a blessing to her husband, you are stepping right into enemy territory, territory he thought he had covered. I love it!

Like any kind of ministry, don't expect the women to fall all over you and thank you and tell you how much this has helped them. Don't let the lack of positive feedback deter you. If you know God wants you to do it, do it. Don't go by the look on their faces.

There have been many months when I didn't want to have the meeting at all. I thought it was a waste of time, only to find out several months later that it really helped. Don't go by your emotions. The devil can work his way in there and drag you down. Concentrate on God and on obeying what He has told you to do. *Always give yourselves fully to the work of the Lord, because you know that your labor in the Lord is not in vain* (1 Corinthians 15:58b NIV).

Expect resistance, but also expect GREAT RESULTS. The strong marriages you foster will advance the kingdom of God!

Let's not wait until there's a BIG problem and a desperate cry for help. Let's not allow another generation learn the hard way! Let's teach women how to take and operate in their strong position as a wife now!

Also I heard the voice of the Lord, saying, Whom shall I send? And who will go for Us? Then said I, Here am I; send me (Isaiah 6:8 NIV).

Note: *For more on mentoring, read* **Mentoring: Confidence in Finding a Mentor and Becoming One** *by Bobb Biehl (Broadman & Holman Publishers, 1996).*

25

Responding to the Battle Cry

A virtuous (chayil) woman is a crown to her husband ....
—Proverbs 12:4a KJV

You and your husband are a team. No matter what you are *specifically* doing to serve the Lord, you are causing people to inherit the promises of God. The instructions and encouragement God gives to you and your husband are the same ones he gave to Joshua. *Be strong (confident) and of good courage, for you shall cause this people to inherit the land which I swore to their fathers to give them* (Joshua 1:6).

The more you're influencing others, the bigger the target you are. The more potential your husband has for accomplishing great things in God's kingdom, the bigger target your marriage is. Whenever you branch out into a new area, start a new ministry, take steps for growth or come into a new level of ministry, expect resistance.

But do not be afraid. You are not of the company of those who shrink back! You are of the company of those who say, "With God we are well able to take the land!" You are in the company of Deborah who obeyed God and against the odds led Israel to a victory over the enemy—Jabin, king of Canaan, and his entire army. ... *and all the army of Sisera fell by the sword, not a man was left* (Judges 4:16).

Do not hold back. Get out on the frontlines. Uphold, push forward, fight for and encourage your husband. Say with me, "I am going to fight with the weapons God gives me. I am going to obey God's commands. I am going to stand strong in the day of trouble. I am going to *hold my position."*

The Lord says your position is strong and secure! (See Proverbs 31:25.) The Lord says, *Have I not commanded you? Be strong, vigorous, and very courageous. Be not afraid, neither be dismayed, for the Lord your God is with you wherever you go* (Joshua 1:9). Almighty God says your marriage is in His hands ... *and there is no one who can deliver out of My hand ...* (Isaiah 43:13).

REMEMBER SARAH?

The Terminator almost destroyed Sarah, but then she heard the battle cry! She realized that she was in a key position. She knew she had to rise up and fight or lie down and die. She decided to rise up and fight.

I love the last scene of the movie. Sarah is in a jeep. Her hair is pulled back and a bandanna is across her forehead. The blade of a large knife on the seat next to her catches the sunlight. She's ready to fight. By the determined look in her eye, you know she's going to win. Sarah heard the battle cry and responded to it.

I believe you hear the battle cry too.

The enemy wants to destroy you and your marriage and your

ministry. He wants to hold back the kingdom of God, but you are not of the company of those who turn back and are destroyed. You are a *chayil* woman. You were chosen for this strong position, for such a time as this, so that the kingdom of God will advance strongly and forcefully.

You hear the battle cry. How will you respond?

Appendix

A Prayer for Your Husband in the Ministry

The Power of the Praying Wife provides prayers for thirty different aspects of your husband's life. However, because it is a book for all wives, it does not have a prayer for your husband as a leader in the kingdom of God. I have provided one here for you. Add on your own scriptures to pray as the Holy Spirit leads you.

A Prayer for Your Husband in the Ministry

Lord, I pray for my husband as a leader in Your kingdom. I pray that he will govern the people well, defend the poor, deliver the children, and crush the oppressor (Psalm 72:2,4). You are not willing that any should perish, but that all should come to repentance (2 Peter 3:9). Because of this, I ask in Jesus' name that ___(husband's name)___ would fully accomplish all that you have set before him to do.

May he use the gifts You've given him to serve others, faithfully administering Your grace. When he speaks, may he be as one speaking the very words of God (1 Peter 4:10,11). In serving, may he have perseverance, steadfastness, goodness, and be full of the Spirit of God. I thank You for fully equipping him to equip others for works of service (Ephesians 4:12).

Show him how to tend, nurture, and guide the flock that You have put in his care willingly, eagerly, and cheerfully. Cause him to be an example of Christian living to the people (1 Peter 5:2). I pray that he will not love the world, neither the things that are in the world, because if he does, Your love will not be in him (1 John 2:15).

Protect him, Lord, from the enemy who would try to hold him back, hold him down, or stop him. I thank You, Lord, for Your Word. It confirms that since You have taught my husband wisdom and led him in uprightness, his steps will not be hampered as he walks, and he will run and shall not stumble (Proverbs 4:11,12).

I thank You that You have begun a good work in my husband and You will complete it (Philippians 1:6). According to Isaiah 46:10, I declare that Your purpose will stand in my husband's life, and that You will do all that You please. In everything my husband does, Lord, may Your kingdom advance, and may You be glorified!